OXFORD

English
An International Approach

Rachel Redford

with Eve Sullivan

OXFORD

UNIVERSITY PRESS

OXFORD
UNIVERSITY PRESS

Great Clarendon Street, Oxford OX2 6DP

Oxford University Press is a department of the University of Oxford.
It furthers the University's objective of excellence in research, scholarship,
and education by publishing worldwide in

Oxford New York

Auckland Cape Town Dar es Salaam Hong Kong Karachi
Kuala Lumpur Madrid Melbourne Mexico City Nairobi
New Delhi Shanghai Taipei Toronto

With offices in

Argentina Austria Brazil Chile Czech Republic France Greece
Guatemala Hungary Italy Japan Poland Portugal Singapore
South Korea Switzerland Thailand Turkey Ukraine Vietnam

British Library Cataloguing in Publication Data

Data available

ISBN: **978-0-19-912666-8**

20 19 18 17

Printed in China

Paper used in the production of this book is a natural, recyclable product made
from wood grown in sustainable forests. The manufacturing process conforms to
the environmental regulations to the country of origin.

Contents

Oxford English: An International Approach, Book 3

Oxford English: An International Approach, Book 3 is the third in a series of four books. The series is aimed at those with English as a first language or a strong second language who are taking English as a subject. The books provide students with a wonderful selection of fiction and non-fiction extracts from across the globe and are grouped into themes such as **'Friendship'**, **'Being free'**, and **'Flying'**.

The unique variety of textual material provides a backdrop against which students can improve their skills in reading, writing, speaking, and listening. Many extracts and activities relate to everyday life and pursuits such as work, education, and travel. This unique mix of content will enable students to learn about their own identity and their place in the world, and to explore the ways in which their personal experience relates to the global picture. The extracts, and the accompanying activities and questions, will encourage students to make these important connections, and to think critically. Many of the issues raised deal with ethical concepts and topics that are of real concern to young people.

The international approach is an important aim of the series. The many unusual and exciting extracts come from all over the world – from New Delhi to New York, Melbourne to Mongolia, Ankara to Africa – to embrace life in the backstreets and canals of a city or the intrepid adventures of those who scale mountains or head off into unknown territories. Readers will delight in the many different points of view that cross cultures and continents, as well as different periods in human history.

A strong focus is placed on writing activities. Often, a writing assignment will come out of a reading activity so that students have a model on which to base their own writing. The writing activities have been designed to motivate students to write, and to expose them to different types of texts. The following useful features support vocabulary development and group discussions.

Wordpool Acquiring vocabulary is an essential part of any learning for both first- and second-language students. An emphasis is placed on encouraging students to identify for themselves the words they need to know. For class discussion, teachers can place large word pools on the blackboard and direct a class activity to identify unknown words from any reading or listening activity. They can be used to review vocabulary and record words recently learned.

Glossary The many glossaries explain technical terms and significant words of cultural relevance. Through this, students will improve their vocabulary and develop an understanding of other cultures.

Word origins Basic etymology and word origins are discussed in this vocabulary feature. Students will begin to understand the development of language and appreciate how languages share vocabulary.

UK /USA English Recognizing the often confusing spellings and differences between the UK and the USA in particular, students are encouraged to pay attention to regional differences in language usage.

Talking points Students will be encouraged to talk with a partner or to discuss topics in groups. Speaking is an important skill in language learning, encouraging students to express opinions and develop a greater appreciation and understanding of a topic, while improving their language skills.

Toolkit Students will learn and be reminded of important language and grammar skills. These are connected to the content and often to the language of a particular extract, so that students can see examples of how the grammar skills work. If students are using the workbook, exercises to practise these skills are provided.

Comprehension Questions are provided to increase students' understanding and comprehension. These questions develop in complexity for deeper understanding and appreciation of the text.

Journals Throughout the units, there are suggested topics for students to write about. Students should write about any aspect of the topic from a personal point of view. They should not be graded on the writing – it is a chance for students to write as a direct form of expression. Students keep these in a separate journal or notebook and teachers can grade students simply by seeing they have filled a page of writing. Journals can be used to link lessons by asking students to share what they have written with the class, perhaps at the start of a lesson. Students often enjoy sharing these because they are based on personal experience or opinion.

The Teacher's Guide: The Teacher's Guide provides lesson plans, rubrics for writing activities and all answers to the student book and the workbook. In addition, there is an audio CD with extracts indicated in the student book with the CD symbol.

The Workbook: An 80-page workbook provides extra practice exercises for vocabulary and grammar, along with additional support for the writing assignments.

And, finally, to acknowledgements. This publication is dedicated to all the students who use this book. It would not have been possible without the permission of the authors and artists who have kindly granted us the rights to reproduce excerpts and illustrations of their work. Special thanks to academic advisor Patricia Mertin, series editor Carolyn Lee, Mara Singer for the design concept and co-author and editor Eve Sullivan.

Rachel Redford, 2010

1 Friendship

What do our friends mean to us?

In this unit you will:

Experience	Read	Create
• psychology	• theories of friendship	• a friendship wall
• philosophy	• poetry	• an e-pal profile
• the United Kingdom	• a web site	• a dialogue
• life on a Native American reservation	• fiction	• an unusual friendship
	• an interview	• journal entries

One old friend is better than two new ones.
Russian proverb

Almost everyone feels the need for friends, although some of us make friends more easily than others. Some of us make friends in childhood, and stay friends for the rest of our lives. Some of us quarrel with our friends and are constantly making new ones. What about you? Do you think that friendships just happen, or do certain factors determine with whom we will become friends? What do you think makes people become friends rather than just acquaintances?

Magazine article

Read what a psychologist says about friendship in a monthly column from a magazine and see if you agree.

Q&A: Friendship

Why do we make the friends we do?

Friends are people who regularly cross our paths, for example our classmates or our team-mates. But why do we become friends with one particular classmate rather than another? Perhaps both our mothers are single parents, or perhaps we are both computer geeks – whatever it is, we have things in common.

How does acquaintanceship develop into friendship?

The key is self-disclosure. 'Can I talk to you for a minute?' or 'May I share something with you?' are questions which could move an acquaintanceship into a friendship. You are taking the risk of disclosing information about yourself, but the acquaintanceship is not going to develop unless there is reciprocity. If your acquaintance listens to what you have to say – perhaps about your problems at home – but does not divulge anything personal in return, there is no reciprocity. That acquaintanceship is not going to tip over into friendship.

Why do some friends stick and others don't?

Having established a friendship through self-disclosure and reciprocity, the glue that binds it is intimacy. This involves emotional expression, and unconditional support, followed by acceptance, loyalty and trust. Our friends are always there for us through thick and thin – but there are limits. If a friend proves to be overcritical of our clothes or our behaviour, the friendship may not last. On the other hand, if our friend asks for help, we will value the friendship more highly.

How do we stay friends?

Four basic behaviours have been identified by psychologists as necessary to maintain the bond of friendship:

1. **Self-disclosure**
2. **Supportiveness**
3. **Interaction**
4. **Keeping the friendship positive**

These first two (self-disclosure and supportiveness) are facilitated by communication. We must be willing to extend ourselves, share our lives, listen, and offer support. Don't worry if you move away – emails and phone calls may be as good as being there. The third (interaction) involves spending time together, while the fourth (keeping the friendship positive) necessitates more consideration of the quality of the relationship. Self-disclosure isn't an unrestricted licence to offload or let off steam. The intimacy which makes a friendship thrive must be enjoyable and nurturing for both of you. The more rewarding a friendship, the better we feel about it and the more willing we are to expend the energy to keep it alive.

Talking points

1 Do you agree with what the psychologist says?

2 Discuss the points in the article which you agree with. Talk about examples of friendships which you have experienced or know about.

3 Are there some points which you do not agree with? For example, if you move to another school do you think it is easy to keep up with your friends from your old school?

4 What 'rules' do you think friends should follow if their friendship is to be enjoyable and nurturing for both of them?

Filling in the friendship wall

Make sure you understand the vocabulary by filling in the gaps in the wall below. All the words appear in the text *Q&A: Friendship*, which you have just read.

Communication is needed to f＿＿＿ two basic behaviours necessary for binding a friendship. (10 letters)

If you tell an acquaintance about an emotional difficulty you are experiencing and he or she does not r＿＿＿, then you are not going to become real friends. (11)

What really makes friends stick together is i＿＿＿. (8)

Within a friendship, friends need to express their e＿＿＿. (8)

A friendship needs to be positive and n＿＿＿ for both of you. (9)

If you are not willing to d＿＿＿ personal details about yourself, you will not develop an acquaintanceship into a friendship. (8)

To be a loyal friend, you need to be s＿＿＿ and be willing to h＿＿＿ your friend if you possibly can. (10 and 4)

You need to maintain the bond of friendship through i＿＿＿, otherwise the friendship will not last. (11)

Not everyone agrees with what p＿＿＿ say. Do you? (13)

Ancient Greek philosophy

From *The Nicomachean Ethics* by Aristotle

Over the centuries, there have been many different theories of friendship. The following extract is by the ancient Greek philosopher Aristotle who lived from 384 BCE to 322 BCE (more than 2,300 years ago). He stated that friendship has three components: 'Friends must enjoy each other's company, they must be useful to one another, and they must share a common commitment to the good'. In contemporary societies, we tend to define friendship in terms of the first component, and define those more useful relationships as something else. But what about the idea of the shared commitment to the 'good'?

✑ Friendship ✑

There are three kinds of friendship:

Friendship based on utility. Utility is an impermanent thing – it changes according to circumstances. Friendships of this kind seem to occur most frequently among those who are pursuing their own advantage. Such persons do not spend much time together, because sometimes they do not even like one another, and therefore feel no need of such an association unless they are mutually useful. So with the disappearance of the grounds for friendship, the friendship also breaks up, because that was what kept it alive. For they take pleasure in each other's company only in so far as they have hopes of advantage from it.

Friendship based on pleasure. Friendship between young people is thought to be grounded on pleasure, because their chief interest is in their own pleasure and the opportunity of the moment. As the years go by, however, their tastes change too, so that they are quick to make and to break friendships; because their affection changes just as the things that please them do. That is why they fall in and out of friendship quickly, changing their attitude often within the same day.

Perfect friendship is based on goodness. Only the friendship of those who are good, and similar in their goodness, is perfect. For these people each alike wish good for the other, and they are good in themselves. And it is those who desire the good of their friends for the friends' sake that are most truly friends, because each loves the other for what he is, and not for any incidental quality. Friendship of this kind is permanent, because in it are united all the attributes that friends ought to have.

ARISTOTLE

Talking points

1 How much pleasure do you derive from friendships based on what you do together?

2 Do you agree with Aristotle's view of friendship among young people?

3 What attributes do you value in yourself and in your friends?

Journal

Write a journal entry about the qualities in a friend that you value most highly. Base it on someone you know.

Poem

From *About Friends* by Brian Jones

In the following poem, the British poet remembers a perfect childhood friendship, and how he felt when he met his friend again after twenty years.

❧ About Friends ☙

The good thing about friends
is not having to finish sentences.

I sat a whole summer afternoon with my friend once
on a river bank, bashing heels on the baked mud
5   and watching the small chunks slide into the water
and listening to them – plop plop plop.
He said, 'I like the twigs when they ... you know ...
like that.' I said, 'There's that branch ...'
We both said, 'Mmmm.' The river flowed and flowed
10 and there were lots of butterflies, that afternoon.

I first thought there was a sad thing about friends
when we met twenty years later.
We both talked hundreds of sentences,
taking care to finish all we said,
15 and explain it all very carefully,
as if we'd been discovered in places
we should not be, and were somehow ashamed.

I understood then what the river meant by flowing.

BRIAN JONES

Comprehension

1 What was so special about the writer's childhood friendship?

2 How had the way they communicated as children changed when the two friends met again twenty years later?

3 In the first part of the poem, the river 'flowed and flowed'. What kind of picture of the scene does this paint for you?

4 In the last line of the poem the flowing of the river has a metaphorical meaning. What is it?

Poem

What do you think the British writer of the following poem has to offer as a friend? How would you describe this type of friendship?

❧ **Friends** ❧

I fear it's very wrong of me,
And yet I must admit,
When someone offers friendship
I want the *whole* of it.
5 I don't want everybody else
To share my friends with me.
At least, I want *one* special one,
Who, indisputably

Likes me much more than all the rest,
10 Who's always on my side,
Who never cares what others say.
Who lets me come and hide
Within his shadow, in his house –
It doesn't matter where –
15 Who lets me simply be myself,
Who's always, *always* there.

Elizabeth Jennings

Comprehension

1 What does the writer want from her friend? Do you think it is 'very wrong' of her to want what she does?

2 What emotional qualities does she have which would make her the sort of friend you would or would not like?

3 Which line or lines in the poem do you most agree with? Quote the words and explain why you have chosen them.

Web page

Online friends, or e-pals, can be a great way to explore new interests, or get to know people from other parts of the world. Read the following requests for e-pals from five fourteen-year-old students in different parts of the world.

Hi, I'm Rob from Florida USA where there's lots of sunshine. What I'm really into is computer games and computers generally. I had my first computer from my mom when I was five and I've been a geek ever since! I've been designing interactive games over the last couple of years and that's what I really want to do big time when I graduate. I'm looking for an e-pal who shares my enthusiasm – or is just as crazy as me! I want to create new games with new ideas from someone from another culture so we can create together. Japan or China would be really cool.

Hi, I'm Rosetta from Singapore. I'm the youngest in a family of five girls. My eldest sister has graduated now and works in an insurance company in the city. My real love in life is fashion and clothes. I'm CRAZY about them. What I do is study the clothes in magazines and on television and I get ideas and design my own things. We have great fabric markets here – Chinese silks and all sorts – so I can afford to look like a beauty queen! I'd like an e-pal who loves fashion and lives somewhere where there are different kinds of fabrics. I'd love to swap ideas and designs. That's what I really want to do with my life – be a designer.

Hi, I'm Jessie from Sweden. I live in a small town on the coast of Sweden. We have been learning English since we were very small at school, so we speak English very well. (I don't want to sound boastful, but we do!) Sometimes I think it's really boring here and I'd love to have an e-pal from far away, like in Africa or China. I want to know what everyday life is like for you. What is your school like? Do you have lots of rules? What do you learn about? What books do you read? Tell me, tell me! I can help you with your English.

Talking points

1 What do you think are the advantages of having a 'virtual' friend?

2 Some people say that chatting to 'virtual' friends on blogs or in on-line chat rooms is a substitute for real life, or even dangerous. Do you agree?

○○○   🗀 email

Hi, I'm Jake from Australia. Just like in all the movies and soaps you've ever seen about Australia, we spend a lot of our lives on the beach surfing and having barbies. But I tell you what really interests me and that's FOOD! I love it. I just love Thai food with all those limes and ginger, and I'd like an e-pal in Thailand. Do you eat just traditional Thai food at home, or do you have fast food like chips and burgers? What do you like best? Do you and your family eat together every day at home? Do you eat outside like us on the beach?

○○○   🗀 email

Hi, I'm Irina from Russia. I live with my mother and four brothers in a town in the east of Russia. Life is not easy here because there used to be a factory here which employed two thousand people, but now it has closed and there is no work. Winter is very long and very cold. Snow is 5 metres high and stays for months. I study hard so that I can learn perfect English and go to Moscow to study when I'm older. I would like an e-pal who I can practise my English with. I would like to talk about your school and the job opportunities in your country. What is your family life like? What do you do in your spare time? I watch movies at home and help my mother with the shopping and housework.

Writing to an e-pal

Be an e-pal. Think about how you want to present yourself and your interests, and your way of life.

- Choose one of these e-pals to reply to. Explain who you are, where you live and tell your e-pal a little about your family life. Give your e-pal the information he or she wants. Ask questions of your own so that your e-pal will have plenty to respond to.
- Write your own request for an e-pal. Include a picture which may be of you, or something which interests you. Include information about yourself, and what you would like from your e-pal.

What happens when friends fall out?

Sometimes friends fall out when their paths diverge or they turn to other people for companionship. It is a part of growing up that people change and move on. Things can come to a head very quickly, as in the following account.

Fiction

From *The Absolutely True Diary of a Part-time Indian* by Sherman Alexie

Junior is a fourteen-year-old boy who feels trapped living on an Indian reservation in Washington State, USA. Eventually, Junior decides he will attend Reardan, the school for white children twenty miles away, and make something of his life. But that means leaving behind his life-long best friend, Rowdy. Junior has to tell Rowdy that he is leaving the reservation school and going to Rearden.

❧ Telling Rowdy ❧

I was the *only* kid, white or Indian, who knew that Charles Dickens wrote *A Tale of Two Cities*. And let me tell you, we Indians were the worst of times and those Reardan kids were the best of times.

5   Those kids were *magnificent*.

They knew *everything*.

And they were *beautiful*.

They were beautiful and smart.

They were beautiful and smart and epic.

10   They were filled with hope.

I don't know if hope is white. But I do know that hope for me is like some mythical creature.

Man, I was scared of those Reardan kids, and maybe I was scared of hope, too, but Rowdy absolutely hated all of it.

15   'Rowdy,' I said. 'I am going to Reardan tomorrow.'

For the first time he saw that I was serious, but he didn't want me to be serious.

> **GLOSSARY**
>
> *The Tale of Two Cities* by Charles Dickens is set at the time of the French Revolution which began in 1789. The famous opening sentence begins: 'It was the best of times, it was the worst of times ...' Junior is thinking of this sentence in line 2.
>
> The **rez** is the reservation where Native American Indians, whose ancestors were the original inhabitants of what became the USA, live separately from the rest of the American population.

'You'll never do it,' he said. 'You're too scared.'

'I'm going,' I said.

20 'No way, you're a wuss.'

'I'm doing it. … I'm going to Reardan tomorrow.'

'You're really serious?'

'Rowdy,' I said. 'I'm as serious as a tumor.'

He coughed and turned away from me. I touched his
25 shoulder. Why did I touch his shoulder? I don't know. I was
stupid. Rowdy spun around and shoved me.

'Don't touch me, you idiot!' he yelled.

My heart broke into fourteen pieces, one for each year that
Rowdy and I had been best friends.

30 I started crying.

That wasn't suprising at all, but Rowdy started crying, too,
and he hated that. He wiped his eyes, stared at his wet hand,
and screamed. I'm sure that everybody on the rez heard that
scream. It was the worst thing I'd ever heard.

35 It was pain, pure pain.

'Rowdy, I'm sorry,' I said. 'I'm sorry.'

He kept screaming.

'You can still come with me,' I said. 'You're still my best
friend.'

40 Rowdy stopped screaming with his mouth but he kept
screaming with his eyes.

'You always thought you were better than me,' he yelled.

'No, no, I don't think I'm better than anybody. I think I'm
worse than everybody else.'

45 'Why are you leaving?'

'I have to go. I'm going to die if I don't leave.'

I touched his shoulder again and Rowdy flinched.

Yes, I touched him again.

What kind of idiot was I?

I was the kind of idiot that got punched hard in the face by
50 his best friend.

Bang! Rowdy punched me.

Bang! I hit the ground.

Bang! My nose bled like a firework.

I stayed on the ground for a long time after Rowdy walked
55 away. I stupidly hoped that time would stand still if I stayed
still. But I had to stand eventually, and when I did, I knew
that my best friend had become my worst enemy.

SHERMAN ALEXIE

Looking closely

1 What is serious about tumours? Find other references to physical pain and injury, used metaphorically.

2 What was Rowdy feeling when he 'kept screaming with his eyes'?

3 How can you tell that despite the fact that he punched his best friend in the face, Rowdy was deeply attached to Junior?

Comprehension

1 Why does the author make the parallel reference to *The Tale of Two Cities*?

2 What is the difference between life on the reservation and Rearden?

3 Why is it important for Junior to go to school in Reardan? What is he leaving behind?

4 What emotions made Rowdy call Junior by all those offensive names? What is likely to happen to their friendship?

5 Why did Junior remain lying on the ground for a while before getting up?

Writing a dialogue

W Think of a reason why you might have to stop seeing so much of a friend who has been important to you. Perhaps you are moving to another part of town, or another city? Perhaps your friend has changed in a way you cannot relate to?

• Write down the dialogue for your imagined conversation as a script or through reported speech.

• What would be the most tactful and least hurtful way of communicating what you need to say to your friend?

Extension reading

From *The Lion, the Witch and the Wardrobe* by C.S. Lewis

In the story, Lucy has just walked through the wardrobe to find herself in the land of Narnia. She is in a forest full of snow, and stands for a while under the lamp-post, before she sees Mr Tumnus, the faun. A faun is a mythological creature that is half human (the top half) and half animal (the bottom half), resembling a goat or a type of deer, with cloven hooves.

In this extract they strike up an unlikely friendship. Notice how Mr Tumnus plays with the word 'Eve' and 'Evening' to refer to Lucy as a 'Daughter of Eve', which means she is human, and a descendant of Eve, the first woman, according to the Bible.

The land of Narnia is home to a number of mythological creatures from the literature of ancient Greece and Rome. Which ones can you identify?

℘ Meeting Mr Tumnus ℘

'Good Evening,' said Lucy. But the Faun was so busy picking up its parcels that at first it did not reply. When it had finished it made her a little bow.

'Good evening, good evening,' said the Faun.
5 'Excuse me – I don't want to be inquisitive – but should I be right in thinking that you are a Daughter of Eve?'

'My name's Lucy,' said she, not quite understanding him.

'But you are – forgive me – you are what they call a girl?'
10 asked the Faun.

'Of course I'm a girl,' said Lucy.

'You are in fact Human?'

'Of course I'm human,' said Lucy, still a little puzzled.

'To be sure, to be sure,' said the Faun. 'How stupid of me!
15 But I've never seen a Son of Adam or a Daughter of Eve before. I am delighted, delighted,' it went on. 'Allow me to introduce myself. My name is Tumnus.'

'I am very pleased to meet you, Mr Tumnus,' said Lucy.

'And may I ask, O Lucy Daughter of Eve,' said Mr Tumnus,
20   'how you have come into Narnia?'

'Narnia? What's that?' said Lucy.

'This is the land of Narnia,' said the Faun, 'where we are
now; all that lies between the lamp-post and the great castle
of Cair Paravel on the eastern sea. And you – you have come
25   from the wild woods of the west?'

'I – I got in through the wardrobe in the spare room,' said
Lucy.

'Ah!' said Mr Tumnus in a rather melancholy voice, 'if only I
had worked harder at geography when I was a little Faun, I
30   should no doubt know all about those strange countries. It is
too late now.'

'But they aren't countries at all, ' said Lucy, almost laughing.
'It's only just back there – at least – I'm not sure. It is
summer there.'

35   'Meanwhile,' said Mr Tumnus, 'it is winter in Narnia, and
has been for ever so long, and we shall both catch cold if we
stand here talking in the snow. Daughter of Eve from the far
land of Spare Oom where eternal summer reigns around the
bright city of War Drobe, how would it be if you came and
40   had tea with me?'

'Thank you very much, Mr Tumnus,' said Lucy. 'But I ought
to be getting back.'

'It's only just round the corner,' said the Faun, 'and there'll be
a roaring fire – and toast – and sardines – and cake.'

45   'Well, it's very kind of you,' said Lucy. 'But I shan't be able to
stay long.'

'If you will take my arm, Daughter of Eve,' said Mr Tumnus,
'I shall be be able to hold the umbrella over both of us.
That's the way. Now – off we go.'

50 And so Lucy found herself walking through the wood arm in arm with this strange creature as if they had known one another all their lives.

They had not gone far before they came to a rocky place with little hills up and little hills down. At the bottom of one
55 small valley Mr Tumnus turned suddenly aside as if he were going to walk straight into an unusually large rock, but at the last moment Lucy found he was leading her into the entrance of a cave. As soon as they were inside she found herself blinking in the light of a wood fire. 'Now we shan't
60 be long,' he said, and immediately put a kettle on.

Lucy thought she had never been in a nicer place. It was a little, dry, clean cave of reddish stone with a carpet on the floor and two little chairs ('one for me and one for a friend,' said Mr Tumnus) and a table and dresser and a mantelpiece
65 over the fire and above that a picture of an old Faun with a grey beard. In one corner there was a door which Lucy thought must lead to Mr Tumnus's bedroom, and on one wall was a shelf full of books. Lucy looked at these while he was setting out the tea things. They had titles like *The Life*
70 *and Letters of Silenus* or *Nymphs and Their Ways* or *Men, Monks and Gamekeepers; a Study in Popular Legend* or *Is Man a Myth?*

'Now, Daughter of Eve! said the Faun.

And really it was a wonderful tea. There was a nice brown
75 egg, lightly boiled, for each of them, and then sardines on toast, and then buttered toast, and then toast with honey, and then a sugar-topped cake. And when Lucy was tired of eating, the Faun began to talk. He had wonderful tales to tell of life in the forest. He told about the midnight dances and
80 how the Nymphs who lived in the wells and the Dryads who lived in the trees came out to dance with the Fauns; about long hunting parties after the milk-white stag who could give you wishes if you caught him; about feasting and treasure-seeking with the wild Red Dwarfs in deep mines and caverns
85 far beneath the forest floor; and then about summer when the woods were green and old Silenus on his fat donkey

would come to visit them, and sometimes Bacchus himself, and the whole forest would give itself up to its jollification for weeks on end.

90 'Not that it isn't always winter now,' he added gloomily. Then to cheer himself up he took out from its case on the dresser a strange little flute that looked as if it were made of straw and began to play. And the tune he played made Lucy want to cry and laugh and dance and go to sleep all at the
95 same time. It must have been hours later when she shook herself and said:

'Oh, Mr Tumnus – I'm so sorry to stop you, and I do love that tune – but really, I must go home. I only meant to stay for a few minutes.'

100 'It's no good *now*, you know,' said the Faun.

'No good?' said Lucy, jumping up and feeling rather frightened. 'What do you mean? I've got to go home at once. The others will be wondering what has happened to me.' But a moment later she asked, 'Mr Tumnus! Whatever is the
105 matter?' for the Faun's brown eyes had filled with tears and then the tears began trickling down its cheeks, and soon they were running off the end of its nose; and at last it covered its face with its hands and began to howl.

'Mr Tumnus! Mr Tumnus!!' said Lucy in great distress.
110 'Don't! don't! What is the matter? Aren't you well? Dear Mr Tumnus, do tell me what is wrong.' But the Faun continued sobbing as if its heart would break. And even when Lucy went over and put her arms round him and lent him her handkerchief, he did not stop. He merely took the
115 handkerchief and kept on using it, wringing it out with both hands whenever it got too wet to be any more use, so that presently Lucy was standing in a damp patch.

'Mr Tumnus!' bawled Lucy in his ear, shaking him. 'Do stop. Stop it at once! You ought to be ashamed of yourself, a great
120 big Faun like you. What on earth are you crying about?'

'Oh – oh – oh!' Sobbed Mr Tumnus, 'I'm crying because I'm such a bad Faun.'

'I don't think you're a bad Faun at all,' said Lucy. 'I think you are a very good Faun. You are the nicest Faun I've ever met.'

125

'Oh – oh – you wouldn't say that if you knew,' replied Mr Tumnus between his sobs. 'No, I'm a bad Faun. I don't suppose there ever was a worse Faun since the beginning of the world.'

130 'But what have you done?' asked Lucy.

'My old father, now,' said Mr Tumnus; 'that's his picture on the mantelpiece. He would never have done a thing like this.'

'A thing like what?' said Lucy.

'Like what I've done,' said the Faun. 'Taken service under the White Witch. That's what I am. I'm in the pay of the White
135 Witch.'

'The White Witch? Who is she?'

'Why, it is she that has got all Narnia under her thumb. It's she that makes it always winter. Always winter and never
140 Christmas; think of that!'

'How awful!' said Lucy. 'But what does she pay *you* for?'

'That's the worst of it,' said Mr Tumnus with a deep groan. 'I'm a kidnapper for her, that's what I am. Look at me, Daughter of Eve. Would you believe that I'm the sort of Faun
145 to meet a poor innocent child in the wood, one that had never done me any harm, and pretend to be friendly with it, and invite it home to my cave, all for the sake of lulling it asleep and then handing it over to the White Witch?'

'No,' said Lucy. 'I'm sure you wouldn't do anything of the
150 sort.'

'But I have,' said the Faun. 'Daughter of Eve, don't you understand? It isn't something I *have* done. I'm doing it now, this very moment.'

'What do you mean?' cried Lucy, turning very white.

155 'You are the child,' said Tumnus. 'I had orders from the White Witch that if ever I saw a Son of Adam or a Daughter of Eve in the wood, I was to catch them and hand them over to her. And you are the first I ever met. And I've pretended to be your
160 friend and asked you to tea, and all the time I've been meaning to wait till you were asleep and then go and tell *Her*.'

'Oh, but you won't, Mr Tumnus,' said Lucy. 'You won't, will you? Indeed, indeed you really
165 mustn't.'

'And if I don't,' said he, beginning to cry again, 'she's sure to find out ... And she'll have my tail cut off, and my horns sawn off, and my beard plucked out, and she'll wave her wand over my
170 beautiful cloven hoofs and turn them into horrid solid hoofs like a wretched horse's. And if she is extra and specially angry she'll turn me into stone and I shall be only a statue of a Faun in her horrible house until the four thrones at Cair
175 Paravel are filled – and goodness knows when that will happen, or whether it will ever happen at all.'

'I'm very sorry, Mr Tumnus,' said Lucy. 'But please let me go home.'

'Of course I will,' said the Faun. 'Of course I've got to. I see
180 that now. I hadn't known what Humans were like before I met you. Of course I can't give you up to the Witch; not now that I know you. But we must be off at once. I'll see you back to the lamp-post. I suppose you can find your own way from there back to Spare Oom and War Drobe?'

185 'I'm sure I can,' said Lucy.

'We must go as quietly as we can,' said Mr Tumnus. 'The whole wood is full of *her* spies. Even some of the trees are on her side.'

They both got up and left the tea things on the table, and Mr Tumnus once more put up his umbrella and gave Lucy his

A statue of a faun

190 arm, and they went out into the snow. The journey back was not at all like the journey to the Faun's cave; they stole along as quickly as they could, without speaking a word, and Mr Tumnus kept to the darkest places. Lucy was relieved when they reached the lamp-post again.

195 'Do you know your way from here, Daughter of Eve?' said Mr Tumnus.

Lucy looked very hard between the trees and could just see in the distance a patch of light that looked like daylight. 'Yes,' she said, 'I can see the wardrobe door.'

200 'Then be off home as quick as you can,' said the Faun, 'and – c-can you ever forgive me for what I meant to do?'

'Why, of course I can,' said Lucy, shaking him heartily by the hand. 'And I do hope you won't get into dreadful trouble on my account.'

205 'Farewell, Daughter of Eve,' said he. 'Perhaps I may keep the handkerchief?'

'Rather!' said Lucy, and then ran towards the far-off patch of daylight as quickly as her legs would carry her.

C.S. Lewis

Comprehension

1 What does Lucy like about Mr Tumnus? What does she find so reassuring about his manners and behaviour?

2 What do 'Spare Oom' and 'War Drobe' stand for? What does Mr Tumnus identify as the most significant difference between the two worlds?

3 What does Lucy find comforting about Mr Tumnus's home?

4 What does Mr Tumnus do to keep Lucy entertained?

5 What dreadful thing has Mr Tumnus done? What does he do to make up for it?

Interview

The following extract is from an interview between the actors Georgie Henley and James McAvoy, who starred in the Walt Disney film version of the novel, *The Chronicles of Narnia: The Lion, the Witch and the Wardrobe*. The two of them discuss the friendship that grew between them in real life, as it did in the story.

When they started filming, Georgie was only ten years old. This was her first acting role.

❧ **Georgie Henley and James McAvoy** ❧

Q: **Why does Lucy follow Mr Tumnus home?**

GEORGIE: She does it because she really trusts in Mr Tumnus. They're almost like long-lost friends, and there's no point in having long-lost friends if you don't go into tea with them.

5

JAMES: The thing that is so special about them is they're nearly the same person in a lot of ways, even though he's 150 and she's eight years old. When they meet each other it is fast friends immediately. It's quite unviable to make friends that quickly, but we have to believe it can happen. But if you can't believe two people can become friends that quickly, then don't watch the rest of the film.

GEORGIE: They connect.

JAMES: Yes, they connect in a really fundamental way, because they're very similar people.

Q: **How did shooting in chronological order help you?**

GEORGIE: We got more mature, really. In the earliest shoots I was a bit of a spitfire on set, I was really hyper on set, wasn't I?

JAMES: You were a bit hyper on set. But I didn't help, I was jumping around like I was seven.

GEORGIE: You were? It did help me.

JAMES: I think so. You guys got more experienced, more chilled out. And you got so much more comfortable by the end.

GEORGIE: And you became more faun-ey. More goat-like.

JAMES: My beard got longer.

GEORGIE: The thing is, when you see a goat, they actually don't curl under like Mr Tumnus', they actually don't go like that. He's already growing a beard, see?

JAMES: I'm starting to. That was my favourite thing, watching you grow. You all grew inches during this film.

10

15

20

25

30

35

GLOSSARY

Here are some examples of colloquial language, frequently used in speech.

A **spitfire**, meaning something or someone who spits fire, describes a person who behaves in an angry or explosive manner.

Hyper, from the Greek word for over or beyond, is often used as a short form of **hyperactive**. This is a medical term for someone who behaves in an overactive or crazy way.

Chilled out means to behave in a relaxed manner, and is related to being 'cool'.

Q:	**Did you keep track on the wall?**	
40	**GEORGIE:**	Yeah. Skandar (Keynes) grew six and a half inches, I did four inches, William (Moseley) grew two inches, and Anna (Popplewell) grew a half an inch.
	Q:	**How did they keep up with your costumes?**
45	**GEORGIE:**	They just ... had to keep doing them again and again and again. It was so weird, do you remember when Will stood up and his fur coat ripped in the back? So wardrobe was, like, seriously stressing, because these were real fur
50		coats.
	Q:	**James, did you want Mr Tumnus to wear a shirt for the coronation?**
	JAMES:	No, he's too scruffy for that, my friend.
	GEORGIE:	Scruffy!
55	**JAMES:**	Well, you know, it's the faun's way, isn't it? Classically speaking, fauns are followers of Dionysus and Bacchus and they make reference to that in the book. They were free, they were unrestricted ... It was all about being
60		open. That's why, I think, it was a good choice to make Tumnus a faun, because he's about openness, which is what he and Lucy have in common.
	Q:	**Did you like filming in New Zealand?**
65	**GEORGIE:**	New Zealand inspired me to write two books on set. One is called 'The Snow Stag,' and one is about an Arctic island, called 'The Pillow of Secrets,' and I sold that to charity and I made about $350 for WWF – not the wrestling
70		fund! The wildlife fund.
	Q:	**Do you want to get them published?**

Journal

Describe a situation in which you got to know someone well, because you had to spend a lot of time together.

GEORGIE: I want to set them up to publish when I'm
older, when I'm a teenager. So I'm going to
keep them safe. And I'm writing a story at the
75 moment called 'The Diary of a Bully,' which
describes a boy who is bullied, and it is a
diary, and it involves the police, and gets quite
serious, and it's an in-depth book. It's quite
disturbing.

80 Q: **What was the hardest thing about filming the movie?**

GEORGIE: Being away from my friends and family.

JAMES: Yeah, being away from my loved ones for so
long. You know, New Zealand is twenty-four
85 hours from London. I couldn't go home for a
few days, it was difficult. It's hard to call.
Emails are the best way.

GEORGIE: Emails and phone calls. And letters. I wrote
letters to school.

An unusual friendship

Write about an unusual or unlikely friendship like that between
Lucy and the faun, or the actors who play them in the film. An
unusual friendship could be between people of very different ages or
backgrounds, Think about what makes your friendship unusual or
special.

- What is the situation that brings the two friends together? What
kinds of things do they do together or have in common?
- Imagine a conversation between the two friends. What do they
talk about?
- Write your conversation down as a narrative, using direct and
indirect speech.

Talking points

1 How does the friendship between the actors help them in their on-screen relationship?
2 Why was this role a particular challenge for Georgie?
3 Discuss in class some of the difficulties of making a film like The Lion, the Witch and the Wardrobe.

Toolkit

Punctuating compound sentences

When joining two main clauses together, a comma is placed before the coordinating conjunction. For example, 'It's quite unviable to make friends that quickly, but we have to believe it can happen.' 'But' is the coordinating conjunction. Find two more compound sentences in the interview above, identify the coordinating conjunction and notice how it has been punctuated. Then write two compound sentences of your own. **W**

2 Education

Why is education so important?

In this unit you will:

Experience
- the United States
- the United Kingdom
- South Africa

Read
- an interview
- a poem
- a play
- autobiography

Create
- an interview
- autobiography
- journals

Learning is a treasure that will follow its owner everywhere.
Chinese proverb

How would your life be different without education? For most of us, it's an essential part of life. This is because we believe that it will help us throughout our lives. 'The mind, once stretched by a new idea, never regains its original dimensions.' This idea was expressed by Oliver Wendell Holmes, Jr. and reflects the idea that education helps us to grow.

Talking points

1 What are some great things you have learned and how did you learn them?

2 What is your idea of a good education?

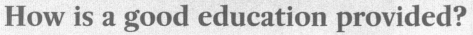

How is a good education provided?

In most parts of the world, providing a good education is seen as essential to society and personal well-being. Although it may not seem like a complicated issue, there are so many different theories and opinions about what is needed to provide a good education. Many people question whether schools need more money, better-educated teachers, formal exams, different types of lessons, more homework or less homework. How important is it for every school-age child to have access to a computer and the Internet? Of course the answers to these questions may be different, according to an individual student's needs and the resources of the local community.

An interview

In the following interview with President Obama, eleven-year-old Damon Weaver from Pahokee in Florida takes the opportunity to raise issues that are close to his heart. The interview took place on 13 August 2009, around the time when the president was due to make a statement on his government's education policies.

Damon had already interviewed a number of prominent people in the United States. Pay attention to his interview techniques.

ᔍ An Interview with President Obama ᔌ

DAMON WEAVER: I've heard that you would like to make an announcement about education. Can you tell me about the announcement?

PRESIDENT OBAMA: Well, Damon, on September 8, when
5   young people around the country have just started or are about to go back to school, I'm going to be making a big speech to people all across the country about the importance of education and the importance of staying in school, about how we want to improve the education system and why it's
10   so important for the country, so I hope everybody tunes in.

WEAVER: All across America, money is being cut from education. How can education be improved with all these cuts?

OBAMA: Well, we here in the administration are actually
15   trying to put more money into schools, and there are a lot of schools all across the country that are getting new buildings and new facilities. We're now putting more money into training good teachers and giving them more support. But money alone is not going to make the difference. We've also
20   got to improve how the schools are operating, and we have been trying to focus on how you identify the best schools and figure out what it is that they're doing well. And we're trying to get other schools that aren't doing so well to do the same kinds of things that the schools who are doing well are

Wordpool

Discuss the meaning of the following words taken from the extract.

facilities [line 17]

funding [26]

reforming [26]

constructive [132]

Make your own wordpool of any other unfamiliar words you come across.

doing. So I hope that we can really see some improvement,
25 not just with funding, but also with reforming how the
schools work.

Can I also add that there are certain programs, like dropout
prevention programs, for example, that local school districts
might not be able to afford, but we can provide federal
30 government funding to those local districts so they can
support such programs.

WEAVER: I've learned that your mom always made sure that
you were doing well at school. What should parents do to
make sure their child's education is better?

35 **OBAMA:** Parents are the most important thing to any child's
ability to do well in school, so making sure you're reading to
your children, especially when they're young, even before
they get to school so they start being used to reading, and
they know their alphabet, they know the basics. So even
40 when they get to kindergarten, they're already a leg up. I
think it's important to make sure that kids are doing their
homework and that they're not just turning on the TV all
day or playing video games. I think parents should talk to
teachers and find out from teachers directly what can be
45 done to improve their child's performance. Setting a high
standard is also important. Saying if you get a B, you can do
better, you can get an A. Making sure we have high
expectations for all children because I think all children can
do well, as long as they have the support that they need.

50 **WEAVER:** Do you have the power to make the school
lunches better?

OBAMA: Well, I remember that when I used to get school
lunches they didn't taste so good, I got to admit. We are
seeing if we can work to at least make school lunches
55 healthier. There's a lot of french fries, pizza, tater tots, all
kinds of stuff that isn't a well-balanced meal, so we want to
make sure there are more fruits and vegetables in the schools.
Now, kids may not end up liking that, but it's better for
them, it'll be healthier for them, and those are some of the
60 changes we're trying to make.

Damon Weaver in Pahokee, Palm
Beach County, Florida

WEAVER: I suggest that we have french fries and mangoes every day for lunch.

OBAMA: See, and if you were planning the lunch program
65 it'd probably taste good to you, but it might not make you big and strong like you need to be. So we want to make sure that food tastes good in school lunches and is healthy for you too.

WEAVER: I looooove mangoes.

OBAMA: I love mangoes too, but I'm not sure we can get
70 mangoes in every school. They only grow in hot temperatures and there are a lot of schools up north where they don't have mango trees.

WEAVER: I notice as president you get bullied a lot. How do you handle it?

75 **OBAMA:** You mean people say mean things about me? I think that when you're president you're responsible for a lot of things. People are having a tough time, they're hurting out there, and the main thing I try to do is just stay focused on trying to do a good job. I understand that sometimes people
80 are going to be mad about things, but if I'm doing a good job – I'm doing my best, and I'm helping people – that keeps me going.

WEAVER: Were you ever bullied in school?

OBAMA: You know, I wasn't bullied too much in school.
85 I was pretty big for my age, but obviously it's a terrible thing and I hope all young people out there understand that they should treat each other with respect.

WEAVER: What can kids do to make our country better?

OBAMA: I think the things that kids can do best is just work
90 really hard in school and succeed. If young people like yourself are reading at high levels, doing their homework, doing math and science and ending up going to college, that makes everyone better off. But also when they have some spare time, try to help people out. It could be people in your

GLOSSARY

A **dropout** is someone who leaves school before graduating high school at age 18.

To **dunk** is a casual term for scoring in basketball by slamming the ball through the hoop.

Dwayne Wade is a basketball celebrity.

A **homeboy** is a close friend or a person from one's hometown.

95　church or your religious community, or out in the neighborhood. Helping an elderly person carry their grocery bags or helping out a younger person with their schoolwork, those kind of things are also really helpful to the country.

WEAVER: Everybody knows that you love basketball. I
100　think it would be cool to have a president who could dunk. Can you dunk?

OBAMA: Not anymore. I used to when I was young, but I'm almost 50 now. Your legs are the first thing to go!

WEAVER: My buddy Dwayne Wade promised me if you
105　gave me the interview he would play you in a one-on-one basketball game. But he's not sure if he would let you score. Would you be willing to play him in a one-on-one basketball game?

OBAMA: I would play Dwayne Wade. I've got to admit,
110　though, Dwayne Wade is a little bit better at basketball than I am, so I would rather have him on my team playing against someone else than play against him.

WEAVER: What is it like to be President of the United States?

115　**OBAMA:** Well, it's very exciting, it's a lot of work, and there are times where you get a little worn down. But every day you have the possibility, the ability to help other people, and if you can do that, it's a great, great thing.

WEAVER: In my town, Pahokee, I've seen a lot of shootings
120　and fights. What are you going to do about violence and to keep me safe?

OBAMA: Well, I think that we have to make sure that all schools have resources to keep kids safe, but also that parents and community members participate in training their
125　young people to resolve arguments and disagreements without resorting to violence. Too many of our young people, they get frustrated or angry with each other, they start acting out in violence. We need to make sure that we're teaching young people to deal with the issues that they may
130　have in a better way, in a more constructive way.

Looking closely

1　How would you describe the language used by Obama and Weaver?

2　Choose a word or phrase that reflects a casual tone. Do you think this is an effective technique? Why or why not?

3　Choose a word or phrase that reflects a more formal tone and discuss how it is or is not effective.

WEAVER: I know that you're busy being the president, but I would like to invite you to my school, Canal Point Elementary School, because there's a lot of good things going on there that I would like you to see.

135 OBAMA: Well I hope that at some point I get a chance to visit your school because you did a great job on this interview! So somebody must be doing something right down at that school.

WEAVER: When I interviewed Vice President Joe Biden, he
140 became my homeboy. Would you like to become my homeboy?

OBAMA: Absolutely, thank you man. Great job.

WEAVER: Thanks for making my dream come true, Mr President.

145 OBAMA: Well I appreciate it. You did an outstanding job. I look forward to seeing you in the future.

Preparing an interview

W Prepare for an interview with a parent, teacher or school principal about education. You might focus on education generally as Weaver did, or issues related to your particular school, or you may want to find out about a person's own experience of education.

- In the interview, Weaver discussed issues that are important to him. What are the major issues that you want to raise?
- Look at Weaver's first questions. They include a statement as well as a question. Be sure to include comments and statements with your interview questions.
- Think about how you can add in some light relief and humour.

Comprehension

1 What are the key issues that Weaver raises and why do you think he chose those specific topics?

2 Why do you think Weaver brings up the topic of school lunches and basketball?

3 Choose one question and one reply and discuss them. Explain why the issue is important and discuss the effectiveness of the question and answer. Give examples.

4 Summarize Obama's key solutions. Do you think they will be effective?

Toolkit

Pronoun and verb contraction
Because the President Obama and Damon Weaver text is a spoken interview, it contains a lot of contractions, for example: 'I've' for 'I have', and 'they're' for 'they are'. These are contractions of a pronoun and a primary verb – the most common kind of contraction in English. Find all of the contractions in the text and work out what words they have been formed from. W

How do we learn in school?

Some students do better than others at school and teachers and educators wonder why. Is the teacher ineffective, or is the school or the type of lesson inappropriate? What can be done to make learning exciting and interesting for all?

Poem

The following poem is a humorous one about a student who is resistant to learning. It also says a lot about the relationship between teachers and students. What do you think makes a good teacher–student relationship?

 ɛɔ Billy McBone ɔ̃

Billy McBone
Had a mind of his own,
Which he mostly kept under his hat.
The teachers all thought
5 That he couldn't be taught,
But Bill didn't seem to mind that.

Billy McBone
Had a mind of his own,
Which the teachers had searched for for years.
10 Trying test after test,
They still never guessed
It was hidden between his ears.

Billy McBone
Had a mind of his own,
15 Which only his friends ever saw.
When the teacher said, 'Bill,
Whereabouts is Brazil?'
He just shuffled and stared at the floor.

Billy McBone
20 Had a mind of his own,
Which he kept under lock and key.
While the teachers in vain
Tried to burgle his brain,
Bill's thoughts were off wandering free.

Allan Ahlberg

Journal

Write down what you enjoy most about school. What would you change about school?

Comprehension

1 What is implied by the phrase 'a mind of his own'?

2 Who is to blame for Billy's refusal to learn? Choose a line that reflects your answer.

3 What comment about education do you think the poet is making?

A play

From *The History Boys* by Alan Bennett

In his play *The History Boys*, playwright Alan Bennett focuses on a select group of sixth-form students, who are being given special coaching to help them get a scholarship to one of the top universities in England. The setting for the play is a boy's school in the north of England, possibly Sheffield or Leeds.

The headmaster wants to get the boys places at the universities of Oxford or Cambridge. 'Oxbridge', short for Oxford and Cambridge, refers to the two oldest and most prestigious universities in England.

In the following selection of scenes from the play, various methods of teaching history and passing exams effectively are discussed among the teachers and students. Not everyone is in agreement. Mrs Lintott and Irwin are teachers. Dakin and Rudge are students.

Christ Church College at the University of Oxford

ᔅᔂ The History Boys ᔂᔃ

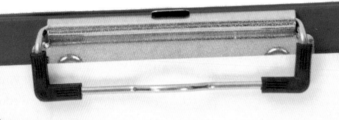

Staff room

Headmaster	Mrs Lintott, Dorothy.
Mrs Lintott	Headmaster?
Headmaster	These Oxbridge boys. Your historians. Any special plans?
Mrs Lintott	Their A Levels are very good.
Headmaster	Their A Levels are very good. And that is thanks to you, Dorothy. We've never had so many. Remarkable! But what now – in teaching terms?
Mrs Lintott	More of the same?
Headmaster	Oh, do you think so?
Mrs Lintott	It's what we've done before.
Headmaster	Quite. Without much success. No one last year. None the year before. When did we last have anyone in history at Oxford and Cambridge?
Mrs Lintott	I tend not to distinguish.
Headmaster	Between Oxford and Cambridge?

Mrs Lintott	Between centres of higher learning. Last year two at Bristol, one at York. The year before …
Headmaster	Yes, yes. I know that, Dorothy. But I am thinking league tables. Open scholarships. Reports to the Governors. I want them to do themselves justice. I want them to do you justice. Factually tip-top as your boys always are, something more is required.
Mrs Lintott	More?
Headmaster	Different. I would call it grooming did that not have overtones of the monkey house. 'Presentation' might be the word.
Mrs Lintott	They know their stuff. Plainly stated and properly organized facts need no presentation, surely.
Headmaster	Oh, Dorothy. I think they do. 'The facts: serving suggestion.'
Mrs Lintott	A sprig of parsley, you mean? …
Headmaster	I am thinking of the boys. Clever, yes, remarkably so. Well taught. But a little … *ordinaire*? Think charm. Think polish. Think Renaissance man.
Mrs Lintott	Yes, Headmaster. …

The teachers

GLOSSARY

The **Advanced Level** General Certificate of Education, universally referred to as an **A Level**, is a qualification offered by educational institutions in the United Kingdom. It is a grading system used to qualify for university entrance.

A **serving suggestion** is a term used in cookery books to suggest attractive ways to present food. When included on food packaging it is used to point out that other ingredients not included in the packet are needed.

A **Renaissance man** is a term used to describe a person who has attained a high level of education across many disciplines.

A **battery chicken** is a form of intensive farming in which the chickens are confined in very small cages, **Free-range** farms allow chickens more space to move around in, with a more varied diet and lifestyle.

Word origins

Oxbridge is a collective term for the universities of Oxford and Cambridge. It can be used as a noun or an adjective, to describe the students who attend them.

School room

Irwin   (distributing exercise books) Dull. Dull. Abysmally dull. A triumph ... the dullest of the lot.

Dakin   I got all the points.

Irwin   I didn't say it was wrong. ...
If you want to learn about Stalin, study Henry VIII. If you want to learn about Margaret Thatcher, study Henry VIII. The wrong end of the stick is the right one ... A question has a front door and a back door. Go in the back, or better still, the side. ... Be perverse.

Take Stalin. Generally agreed to be a monster, and rightly. ... Find something, anything, to say in his defence. History nowadays is not a matter of conviction. It's a performance. It's entertainment. And if it isn't, make it so. ...

Rudge   I get it. It's an angle. You want us to find an angle.

The boys

Looking closely

1 Why does Mrs Lintott make the comparison of the new teaching methods to 'a sprig of parsley'?

2 Which word in the text sums up Irwin's idea of taking a new approach to accepted historical facts? What other metaphor does he use?

3 How does Rudge sum up this new approach?

4 Explain the metaphor used in the third extract to compare the two different approaches to learning with chicken farming.

School corridor

Mrs Lintott	Ah, Rudge.
Rudge	Miss.
Mrs Lintott	How are you getting on with Mr Irwin?
Rudge	It's … interesting Miss, if you know what I mean. It makes me grateful to you for your lessons.
Mrs Lintott	Really? That's nice to hear.
Rudge	Firm foundations type thing. Point A. Point B. Point C. Mr Irwin is more … free-range?
Mrs Lintott	I hadn't thought of you as a battery chicken, Rudge.
Rudge	It's only a metaphor, Miss.
Mrs Lintott	I'm relieved to hear it.
Rudge	You've force-fed us the facts; now we're in the process of running around acquiring flavour.
Mrs Lintott	Is that what Mr Irwin says?
Rudge	Oh no, Miss. The metaphor's mine.

Comprehension

1 What is wrong with being 'ordinaire' ? What does the headmaster want to achieve with his students?

2 What new approaches to history is Irwin trying to encourage?

3 How does Rudge complement his former teacher Mrs Lintott? What does he prefer about her teaching methods?

4 What does Irwin suggest is needed to get the attention of the university examiners?

Talking points

1 Have you heard of the phrase 'A little information goes a long way.'? How does this apply to some of the ideas raised in these extracts from *The History Boys*?

2 Discuss, in your group, connections you could make between different countries and different periods in history.

How do we learn outside school?

Much of what we learn is from experience, from everyday life. Our family life, friends and the things that happen to us and the things we observe tell us a lot about the world. These experiences and observations are sometimes recounted in people's autobiographies. Autobiographical accounts can be as touching and moving as novels and poetry, as they often contain descriptions and experiences that are genuine and heartfelt.

Autobiography

From *My Early Days*, by Nelson Mandela

Nelson Mandela is one of the most important leaders of the modern age. He was born in a village in Transkei, about 550 miles south of Johannesburg in South Africa, where most children did not go to school.

In 1994, at the age of seventy-six, Mandela became South Africa's first-ever black President, following the country's first-ever multi-racial elections. During his lifetime, Mandela endured twenty-seven years in prison for his anti-government activities, and it was in prison that he began to write his autobiography from which the following text is taken. Despite his great age and his retirement in 2004, Mandela has continued to work towards justice and peace in the world.

Wordpool

dung [line 7]

ochre [14]

poplar [17]

dipping tank [19]

slingshot [28]

udder [30]

to get the hang of [43]

unruly [44]

Part of a Xhosa village in Transkei, South Africa

❧ My Early Days ❧

My home village of Qunu was situated in a narrow, grassy valley criss-crossed by clear streams, and overlooked by green hills. It consisted of no more than a few hundred people who lived in huts, which were beehive-shaped

5   structures of mud walls, with a wooden pole in the centre holding up a peaked grass roof. The floor was kept smooth by smearing it regularly with fresh cow dung. The smoke from the hearth escaped through the roof, and the only opening was a low doorway one had to stoop to walk

10 through. The huts were generally grouped in a residential area that was some distance away from the maize fields. There were no roads, only paths through the grass worn away by barefooted boys and women. The women and children of the village wore blankets dyed in ochre. Cattle,

15 sheep, goats and horses grazed together in common pastures. The land around Qunu was mostly treeless except for a cluster of poplars on a hill overlooking the village. In the area, there were two small primary schools, a general store, and a dipping tank to rid the cattle of ticks and diseases.

20 From an early age, I spent most of my free time in the veld playing and fighting with the other boys of the village. At night, I shared my food and blanket with these same boys. I was no more than five when I became a herd-boy looking after sheep and calves in the fields. I discovered the almost

25 mystical attachment that the Xhosa have for cattle, not only as a source of food and wealth, but as a blessing from God and a source of happiness. It was in the fields that I learned how to knock birds out of the sky with a slingshot, to gather wild honey and fruits and edible roots, to drink warm, sweet

30 milk straight from the udder of a cow, to swim in the clear, cold streams, and to catch fish with string and sharpened bits of wire. From these days I date my love of the veld, of open spaces, the simple beauties of nature, the clean line of the horizon.

35 As boys, we were mostly left to our own devices. We played with toys we made ourselves. We moulded animals and birds

Journal

Think of a favourite game you played as a child. Describe the game, how you played, and who you played with. Did this game teach you a lesson for life? If so, what was it?

Looking closely

1   Explain what 'dyed in ochre' means. [line 14]

2   Explain the 'mystical attachment' which the Xhosa had for their cattle.

3   What is meant by the following in your own words: *a*) 'left to our own devices' (line 35) *b*) 'Nature was our playground' (line 38) *c*) 'I had lost face' (lines 50–51)?

4   What reason did Mandela's father give for agreeing to his son going to school?

5   What does the last sentence tell you about Mandela as a boy and as a man?

Nelson Mandela at home in Qunu on his 90th birthday in 2008

Comprehension

1 How did the village boys entertain themselves? Would you have enjoyed this life? Why or why not?

2 What did Mandela learn during his early life and how did he learn? How valuable do you think his learning was?

3 What important lesson did he learn from the donkey? How valuable do you think the lesson was to him as an adult?

4 Explain how it was that Mandela went to school even though no member of his family had done so before.

out of clay. We made ox-drawn sledges out of tree branches. Nature was our playground. The hills above Qunu were dotted with large smooth rocks which we transformed into
40 our own roller-coaster. We sat on flat stones and slid down the face of the large rocks. I learned to ride by sitting on top of calves – after being thrown to the ground several times, one got the hang of it.

I learned my lesson one day from an unruly donkey. We had
45 been taking turns climbing up and down its back and when my chance came, I jumped on, and the donkey bolted into a nearby thorn bush. It bent its head, trying to unseat me, which it did, but not before the thorns had pricked and scratched my face, embarrassing me in front of my friends.
50 Africans have a highly developed sense of dignity. I had lost face among my friends. Even though it was a donkey that unseated me, I learned that to humiliate another person is to make him suffer an unnecessarily cruel fate. Even as a boy, I defeated my opponents without dishonouring them.

55 The Mbekela brothers would often see me playing or minding sheep and come over to talk to me. One day, George

Mbekela paid a visit to my mother. 'Your son is a clever young fellow,' he said. 'He should go to school.' My mother remained silent. No
60 one in my family had ever attended school and my mother was unprepared for Mbekela's suggestion. But she did relay it to my father who, despite – or perhaps because of – his own lack of education, immediately
65 decided that his youngest son should go to school.

The schoolhouse consisted of a single room, with a Western-style roof, on the other side of the hill from Qunu. I was seven years old,
70 and on the day before I was to begin, my father took me aside and told me that I must be dressed properly for school. Until that time, I, like all the other boys in Qunu, had worn only a blanket, which was wrapped round one shoulder and pinned at the waist. My
75 father took a pair of his trousers and cut them at the knee. He told me to put them on, which I did, and they were roughly the correct length, although the waist was far too large. My father then took a piece of string and drew the trousers in at the waist. I must have been a comical sight, but
80 I have never owned a suit I was prouder to wear than my father's cut-off trousers.

NELSON MANDELA

Talking points

1 What did young Mandela learn before he went to school?

2 Can you think of an experience you had as a young child which taught you a lesson the hard way? Tell the group about it.

w Writing autobiography

Write a short autobiography about your early school days. You can focus on one particular day or on general memories of your first weeks.

- Make a list of everything you can remember. Then see if there are a few specific things you could focus on in your account.
- Write about how you felt, and what kind of child you were. Think about how those early memories reflect who you are today.

Extension reading

From *To Sir With Love* by E.R. Braithwaite

E.R. Braithwaite worked in the 1950s as a teacher in the East End of London. With an Oxford education behind him, but no formal training as a teacher, he was placed in charge of an undisciplined class of final-year students. As a black man, working in a school with a predominantly white, working-class population, with little or no aspiration to higher learning, he had his job cut out for him. After the first clashes with this badly behaved and defiant class, one morning, in desperation, he tries to win their trust and cooperation by talking to them frankly about what he wants them to achieve together.

✂ **My Plans For This Class** ✂

'I am your teacher, and I think it right and proper that I should let you know something of my plans for this class.' I tried to pitch my voice into its most informally pleasant register. 'We're going to talk, you and I, but we'll be
5   reasonable with each other. I would like you to listen to me without interrupting in any way, and when I'm through any one of you may say your piece without interruption from me.' I was making it up as I went along and watching them; at the least sign that it wouldn't work I'd drop it, fast.

10   They were interested, in spite of themselves; even the husky, blasé Denham was leaning forward on his desk watching me.

'My business here is to teach you, and I shall do my best to make my teaching as interesting as possible. If at any time I say anything which you do not understand or with which
15   you do not agree, I would be pleased if you would let me know. Most of you will be leaving school within six months or so; that means that in a short while you will be embarked on the very adult business of earning a living. Bearing that in mind, I have decided that from now on you will be treated,
20   not as children, but as young men and women, by me and by each other. When we move out of the state of childhood certain higher standards of conduct are expected of us ...'

Wordpool

informally [line 3]

husky [10]

blasé [11]

to embark [17]

to barge in [33]

insolently [34]

courtesies [44]

conduct [100]

How long does it take?

In the days of journeymen workers, a day trip meant covering a short distance on foot. These days, it is possible to travel by aeroplane to the other side of the world in one day (24 hours).

When the French writer Jules Verne wrote *Around the World in Eighty Days*, a novel set in 1872, he was being very modern and very bold to boast that the distance could be covered in eighty days. Already, in the late nineteenth century, he suggests 'The world has grown smaller, since a man can now go round it ten times more quickly than a hundred years ago.' To prove this, he provided the following travel itinerary (also marked on the map provided below):

From London to Suez via Mont Cenis and Brindisi, by rail and steamboat	7 days
From Suez to Bombay, by steamboat	13 days
From Bombay to Calcutta, by rail	3 days
From Calcutta to Hong Kong, by steamboat	13 days
From Hong Kong to Yokohama (Japan), by steamboat	6 days
From Yokohama to San Francisco, by steamboat	22 days
From San Francisco to New York, by rail	7 days
From New York to London, by steamboat and rail	9 days
Total	80 days

Word origins

Journey comes from the Old French *jornee* (modern French *journée*), meaning work or distance completed in a day. (*Le jour* is modern French for 'day'.)

A *journeyman* was someone who was hired for a day's work.

Caricature of Jules Verne, author of *Around the World in Eighty Days*, with a model of the globe speared by his writer's quill pen

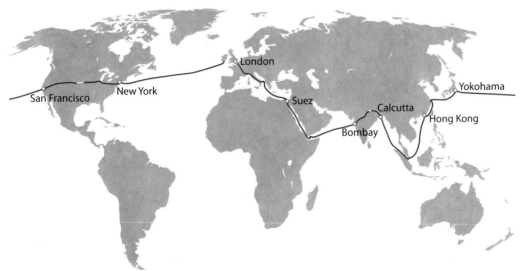

The route taken by Phileas Fogg in *Around the World in Eighty Days* by Jules Verne.

Fiction

From *Around the World in Eighty Days* by Jules Verne

In the following extract from the novel *Around the World in Eighty Days*, Phileas Fogg has just returned home early from the Reform Club to his house at number 7, Savile Row, Burlington Gardens, in London. He has taken on a bet for £20,000 with his fellow club members, to travel around the world in eighty days.

Passepartout, his French servant, is shocked to see his master home so early. It is his first day in this new position of employment, and he was looking forward to a restful life as Fogg is known for his regular habits. Passepartout is even more shocked when he hears that they are due to travel to the English port of Dover, to cross the English Channel by boat to Calais in France that very evening.

Phileas Fogg arrives home early

Passepartout, his servant

๛ In which Phileas Fogg Astounds ๛ Passepartout, his Servant

Having won twenty guineas at whist, and taken leave of his friends, Phileas Fogg, at twenty-five minutes past seven, left the Reform Club.

5 Passepartout, who had studied the programme of his duties, was more than surprised to see his master guilty of the inexactness of appearing at this unaccustomed hour; for, according to the rule, he was not due in Saville Row until precisely midnight.

Mr. Fogg went to his bedroom, and called out,

10 'Passepartout!'

Passepartout did not reply. It was not the right hour.

'Passepartout!' repeated Mr. Fogg, without raising his voice.

Passepartout made his appearance.

'I've called you twice,' observed his master.

15 'But it is not midnight,' responded the other, showing his watch.

'I know it; I don't blame you. We start for Dover and Calais in ten minutes.'

20 A puzzled grin spread over Passepartout's round face; clearly he had not understood his master.

'Monsieur is going to leave home?'

'Yes,' returned Phileas Fogg. 'We are going round the world.'

Passepartout opened his eyes wide, raised his eyebrows, held up his hands, and seemed about to collapse, so overcome
25 was he with astonishment.

'Round the world!' he murmured.

'In eighty days,' responded Mr. Fogg. 'So we haven't a moment to lose.'

'But the trunks?' gasped Passepartout, unconsciously
30 swaying his head from right to left.

'We'll have no trunks; only a carpet-bag, with two shirts and three pairs of stockings for me, and the same for you. We'll buy our clothes on the way. Bring down my mackintosh and travelling-cloak, and some stout shoes, though we shall do
35 little walking. Make haste!'

Passepartout tried to reply, but could not. He went up to his own room, fell into a chair, and muttered: 'That's good, that is! And all I wanted was a quiet life!'

He mechanically set about making the preparations for
40 departure. Around the world in eighty days! Was his master a fool? No. Was this a joke, then? They were going to Dover; good! To Calais; good again! After all, Passepartout, who had been away from France five years, would not be sorry to set foot on his native soil again. Perhaps they would go as far
45 as Paris, and it would do his eyes good to see Paris once more. But surely a gentleman unwilling to take so many steps would stop there; no doubt – but, then, it was nonetheless true that he was going away, this person who had previously had such an orderly domestic life!

Word origins

Passepartout is from the French *passe-partout*, from *passer* 'to pass' and partout 'everywhere', and means a master key. It is also related to the French word for passport.

Alms from *alemosyna* in Church Latin (*eleemosyne* in Greek), are a form of charitable giving. To give or ask for alms is to request or show pity or mercy.

50 By eight o'clock Passepartout had packed the modest carpet-bag, then, still troubled in mind, he carefully shut the door of his room, and descended the stairs to Mr. Fogg.

Mr. Fogg was quite ready. Under his arm might have been observed a red-bound copy of Bradshaw's Continental
55 Railway Steam Transit and General Guide, with its timetables showing the arrival and departure of steamboats and railways. He took the carpet-bag, opened it, and slipped into it a goodly roll of Bank of England notes, which would pass wherever he might go.

60 'You have forgotten nothing?' asked he.

'Nothing, monsieur.'

'My mackintosh and cloak?'

'Here they are.'

'Good! Take this carpet-bag,' handing it back to
65 Passepartout. 'Take good care of it, for there are twenty thousand pounds in it.'

Passepartout nearly dropped the bag, as if the twenty thousand pounds were in gold, and weighed him down.

Master and man then descended, the street-door was double-
70 locked, and at the end of Saville Row they took a cab and drove rapidly to Charing Cross. The cab stopped before the railway station at twenty minutes past eight. Passepartout jumped off the box and followed his master, who, after paying the cabman, was about to enter the station, when a
75 poor beggar-woman, with a child in her arms, her naked feet smeared with mud, her head covered with a wretched bonnet, from which hung a tattered feather, and her shoulders wrapped in a ragged shawl, approached, and mournfully asked for alms.

80 Mr. Fogg took out the twenty guineas he had just won at whist, and handed them to the beggar, saying, 'Here, my good woman — I'm glad that I met you;' and passed on.

Looking closely

1 What is Phileas Fogg guilty of in Passepartout's eyes at the beginning of the extract?

2 Find the phrase that states what Passepartout expected of life with his new employer.

3 Throughout the extract Phileas expresses little emotion. We get a more detailed account of Passepartout's emotional state. Select key words and phrases that describe how Passepartout was feeling.

4 Find examples in the text of precise times at which the actions occur. Construct a brief timeline of the events in the extract.

Passepartout had a moist sensation about the eyes; his master's action touched his heart.

85 Two first-class tickets for Paris having been speedily purchased, Mr. Fogg was crossing the station to the train, when he saw his five friends from the Reform Club.

'Well, gentlemen,' said he, 'I'm off, you see; and, if you will examine my passport when I get back, you will be able to
90 judge whether I have accomplished the journey agreed upon.'

'Oh, that would be quite unnecessary, Mr. Fogg,' said Ralph politely. 'We will trust your word, as a gentleman of honour.'

'You do not forget when you are due in London again?' asked Stuart.

95 'In eighty days; on Saturday, the 21st of December, 1872, at a quarter before nine p.m. Good-bye, gentlemen.'

Phileas Fogg and his servant seated themselves in a first-class carriage at twenty minutes before nine; five minutes later the whistle screamed, and the train slowly glided out of the
100 station.

The night was dark, and a fine, steady rain was falling. Phileas Fogg, snugly sitting in his corner, did not open his lips. Passepartout, not yet recovered from the shock of it all, clung mechanically to the carpet-bag, with its enormous
105 treasure.

Just as the train was whirling through Sydenham, Passepartout suddenly uttered a cry of despair.

'What's the matter?' asked Mr. Fogg.

'Alas! In my hurry – I – I forgot –'

110 'What?'

'To turn off the gas in my room!'

'Very well, young man,' returned Mr. Fogg, coolly, 'it will burn – at your expense.'

JULES VERNE

Charing Cross Station, London, in 1874

Comprehension

1 Describe Phileas's mood as he tells Passepartout his plans.

2 What essential items does Phileas take with him on his journey?

3 What is the significance of Phileas's act of charity at Charing Cross Station?

4 What did Passepartout forget?

5 In what ways is Phileas Fogg a caricature of an English gentleman?

Journal

Write a journal entry about setting off on a journey. Give precise details of your itinerary and what you took with you.

Travel Writing

From *A Lady's Life in the Rocky Mountains* by Isabella Bird

In 1873, Isabella Bird, an adventurer from England, rode a horse 800 miles through the Rocky Mountains in the Western United States. She wrote letters home to her sister so that she could imagine all of Isabella's adventures in detail. Magazines and newspapers in England and the United States began buying her letters and publishing them, which provided her with money to continue travelling throughout the world. She became well known for her writing and she found she was happiest when exploring exciting places.

✆ ∽ Finding our Way through the Dark ∾

After riding twenty miles, which made the distance for that day fifty, I remounted Birdie to ride six miles farther, to a house which had been mentioned to me as a stopping-place. The road rose to a height of 11,000 feet, and from thence I
5 looked my last at the lonely, uplifted prairie sea. 'Denver stage-road!' The worst, rudest, dismallest, darkest road I have yet travelled on, nothing but a winding ravine, the Platte Canyon, pine-crowded and pine-darkened, walled in on both sides for six miles by pine-skirted mountains 12,000
10 feet high! Along this abyss for forty miles there are said to be only five houses, and were it not for miners going down, and freight-waggons going up, the solitude would be awful. As it

90   worry, we will find something to eat, you'll see. This
     country's different from ours, so we gotta learn to find their
     bush tucker, that's all. Come on, let's go along now.'

     Molly managed to coax Gracie out of her stubbornness and
     they walked briskly to where Daisy sat playing with some
95   dry banksia nuts. She stood up when she saw them coming
     and the three of them walked northwards.

     The skies were grey and a cold wind was blowing across the
     bushland. It looked like more rain was coming their way.
     Gracie and Daisy missed their warm gabardine coats and
100 they longed for a meal of meat, hot damper and sweet tea.
     They continued north, through the wet countryside, never
     knowing what was waiting for them over the next hill.

     The three were pacing in good style, covering the miles in an
     easy manner. Soon they found that they were entering a
105 landscape dominated by clumps of grass trees. Interspersed
     amongst them were zamia palms and scattered here and
     there were a few marri, wandoo and mallee gums. The girls
     descended a hill into a clump of tall flooded river gums and
     paperbarks and stared at the flowing water. They had come
110 to a branch of the Moore River.

     'How are we going to get across the river, Dgudu?' asked
     Daisy.

     'I don't know yet,' she replied as she began to search along
     the banks until she found a suitable place to cross.

115 'Up here,' she called out to her sisters. 'We will cross over
     on this fence. Come on,' encouraged Molly as she tucked
     her dress into the waist of her bloomers. With her calico
     bag slung around her neck, she clung to the top strand of
     fence wire, with her feet planted firmly on the bottom
120 strand.

     'See, it's strong enough to hold us,' she assured them.
     'Watch me and follow, come on.'

     Slowly and gingerly they stepped onto the fence wire, not
     daring to look down at the brown flooded river below.

Banksia seed pod

Paperbark trees

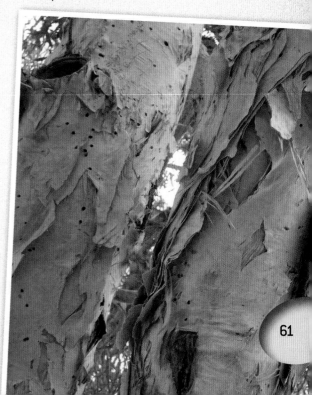

61

125 The water swirled and splashed against their feet. They tried to shut out the sounds and sights of the gushing water and concentrated on reaching the muddy bank on the other side. They were worried about their precious bags that contained all their worldly goods, which wasn't much at all, just an
130 extra pair of bloomers, a frock, their small mirrors, combs and a cake of Lifebuoy soap. However, they made it safely.

On their second day they came into a section of bushland that had been ravaged by fire. All the trees and the grass under them was burnt black. In a few weeks' time, however,
135 this charcoal landscape would be revived by the rain. It would come alive and be a green wilderness again, full of beautiful flowers and animals that are wonderfully and uniquely Australian. The three girls walked in silence over the next hill where they saw a most unexpected but very
140 welcome sight indeed. Coming towards them were two Mardu men on their way home from a hunting trip. Gracie and Daisy were so pleased to see them that they almost ran to meet them, but Molly held the girls back and whispered softly, 'Wait.'

145 So the three girls waited for the men to come closer. When they saw the men's catch, they drooled – a cooked kangaroo and two murrandus. The girls were more interested in the bush tucker than in the two hunters who introduced themselves and told the girls that they were from Marble Bar.

150 'Where are you girls going?' asked one of the men.

'We are running away back home to Jigalong,' replied Molly.

'Well, you girls want to be careful, this country different from ours, you know,' advised the old man with the white hair and a bushy white beard.

155 'They got a Mardu policeman, a proper cheeky fullah. He flog 'em young gel runaway gels like you three,' he added very concerned for them as they were from the Pilbara too.

'Youay,' said Molly. 'We heard about him at the settlement.'

A goanna (*murrundu*) on a tree trunk

Looking closely

1 1 There are many Aboriginal and colloquial English expressions in this story. Identify the standard English words for: 'gunna', 'gotta' and 'fullah'.

2 What are 'bloomers'? What other 'worldly goods' did they take with them? Which world do these refer to?

3 The narrator identifies a range of bush habitats (environments) and species of plants. Describe the different landscapes in your own words.

4 Find the phrase used to identify what will happen to the charcoal landscape in a few weeks' time.

'He follow runaway gels and take 'em back to the settlement.
He's a good tracker, that Mardu,' the old man told them.

'We know that, the girl from Port Hedland already told us
about him,' replied Molly who was confident that the black
tracker would not be able to follow their path because their
footprints would have been washed away by the rain.

The men gave them a kangaroo tail and one of the goannas.
They shook hands with the girls and turned to walk away
when the younger man remembered something.

'Here, you will need these,' he said as he held up a box of
matches. Then he emptied another box and filled it with salt.

The girls thanked them and said goodbye.

'Don't forget now, go quickly. That Kimberley bloke will be
looking for you right now, this time now.'

It was highly unlikely that an attempt to track them down in
this weather would even be considered but Molly wasn't
taking any chances.

The miles they had covered should have been adequate
according to Daisy and Gracie, but no, their elder sister
made them trudge along until dusk. Then the three young
girls set about preparing a wuungku made from branches of
trees and shrubs. They searched under the thick bushes and
gathered up handfuls of dry twigs and enough leaves to start
a small fire. There was no shortage of trees and bushes
around their shelter as they grew in abundance, quite
different from the sparse landscape of the Western Desert.
Each girl carried armfuls of wood and dropped them on the
ground near the fire to dry, as they had decided that it was
safe enough to keep the fire burning all night. They made the
fire in a hole in the ground in the centre of the shelter.

After a supper of kangaroo tail, goanna and the last crust of
bread, washed down with rain water, they loaded more
wood on the fire and slept warm and snug in the rough bush
shelter around the fire.

DORIS PILKINGTON (NUGI GARIMARA)

Comprehension

1 What kind of shelters do the girls sleep in? Explain why they chose these particular types of shelter on their first two nights.

2 Why can't the girls eat the rabbit that Gracie has killed?

3 What do they need to learn about to make sure they have enough to eat?

4 The girls face a number of challenges to make their way home safely. What are they particularly scared of?

5 The black tracker is from the Kimberley, a region close to the Pilbara where the girls come from. Why does this make him a particular threat?

Work

How do we view people's working lives?

In this unit you will:

Experience
- the United Kingdom
- the United States

Read
- autobiography
- a profile
- fiction
- an interview

Create
- a journal entry
- a job profile
- a research presentation

Work! work! work!
While the cock is crowing aloof!
And work – work – work,
Till the stars shine through the roof!

From 'The Song of the Shirt' by Thomas Hood, 1843

Work, work, work! All adults need paid employment in order to earn a living to support themselves and their families. In the opening quotation, Thomas Hood shows sympathy for the nineteenth-century seamstresses, who spent many long daylight and night-time hours sewing garments for a meagre wage.

Talking points

1 How are people defined by the work they do?
2 Why is work so important to our daily lives?

What are the working conditions like?

People all over the world, and over the centuries, have experienced very different working conditions. Some people, like the nineteenth-century seamstress in the poem, work from home. Other people go to an office every day. Many people work in very challenging environments. Can you think of a working environment today as dramatic as the one in this picture?

Journal

Describe a workplace you know about.

The Wealth of England: The Bessemer Converter, painted by William Holt Yates Titcomb in 1895

The Bessemer Converter was one of the great industrial inventions of the late nineteenth century. It converted iron into steel. The year that William Holt Yates Titcomb painted this picture, Britain was exporting a million tons of steel around the world.

Imagine what it must have been like to be one of those men stoking the machine with coal and handling the great vats of molten metal. How does it compare with the modern industrial scene illustrated here?

Autobiography

From *Kitchen Confidential* by Anthony Bourdain

Many people work with noisy or dangerous machines, or in environments that generate extreme heat. The following extract from an autobiography of a chef who became a writer describes what it was like to work in the kitchen of a top restaurant in New York.

✌ The Kitchen ✌

On the strength of my diploma – and my willingness to work for peanuts – I landed a job almost right away at the venerable New York institution, the Rainbow Room, high at the top of the Rockefeller Center. It was my first experience
5 of the real Big Time, one of the biggest, busiest and best-known restaurants in the country. I was willing to do anything to prove myself, and when I got in that elevator to the sixty-fourth-floor kitchen for the first time, I felt as if I was blasting off to the moon.

10 The Rainbow Room at that time sat a little over 200 people. The Rainbow Grill sat about another 150. Added to that were two lounges where food was available, *and* an entire floor of banquet rooms – all of it serviced simultaneously by

A kitchen in a top New York restaurant

a single, central kitchen. So you had some major league
15 volume, as well as some major league cooks to go along
with it.

A long hot line of glowing flat-tops ran along one wall,
flames actually roaring back up into a fire wall behind them.
A few feet across, separated by a narrow, trench-like
20 workspace, ran an equally long stainless-steel counter. Much
of this counter was taken up by vast, open steam boilers
which were kept at a constant, rolling boil. What the cooks
had to contend with was a long, uninterrupted slot, with no
air circulation, with nearly unbearable dry, radiant heat on
25 one side and clouds of wet steam heat on the other. When I
say unbearable, I mean they couldn't bear it; cooks would
regularly pass out and have to be dragged off to recuperate.

There was so much heat coming off those ranges – especially
when the center rings were lit for direct fire – that the filters
30 in the overhead hoods would often burst into flames,
inspiring a somewhat comical scene as the overweight Italian
chef would hurl himself down the narrow line with a fire
extinguisher, bowling over the cooks and tripping as he
hurried to put out the flames before the central system went
35 off and filled the entire kitchen with fire-suppressant foam.

As I've said, it was hot. Ten minutes into the shift, the cheap
polyester whites we all wore would be soaked through with
sweat, clinging to chest and back. All the cooks' necks and
wrists were pink and inflamed with awful heat rashes. It was
40 a madhouse.

ANTHONY BOURDAIN

UK	USA
centre	center
lift	elevator

As the Rockefeller Center is an American institution, it is always spelt this way.

Looking closely

1 What do you think the writer means by 'major league'? What adjective could you use in its place?

2 In what way was the employees' workspace 'trench-like'?

3 Provide an alternative word or phrase for the following words from the text: 'venerable', 'simultaneously', 'rolling', 'radiant', 'bowling'.

4 What does the writer mean by saying 'I felt as if I was blasting off to the moon.' How was he feeling when he got into the lift of the Rockefeller Center?

Comprehension

1 How does the writer feel about his new job?

2 What were the sources of the 'radiant heat' on one side and the 'wet steam heat' on the other?

3 In what way was this heat literally 'unbearable' for some of the employees?

4 What was 'comical' about the scene of the chef and his fire extinguisher?

mill is work, while rolling ten-pins or climbing Mont Blanc is only amusement. There are wealthy gentlemen in England

95 who drive four-horse passenger-coaches twenty or thirty miles on a daily line, in the summer, because the privilege costs them considerable money; but if they were offered wages for the service, that would turn it into work and then they would resign.

100 The boy thought about the substantial change which had taken place in his worldly circumstances, and then wended toward headquarters to report.

MARK TWAIN

Mark Twain's boyhood home and Tom Sawyer fence in the town of Hannibal, Missouri, USA

Comprehension

1 Why does Tom take his time before saying to Ben 'Why it's you, Ben! I warn't noticing'?

2 How does Tom trick Ben?

3 What substantial change has taken place in Tom's worldly status by the end of the extract?

4 What is the essential lesson Tom learns about how to get the most out of people?

5 What does the phrase 'wended toward headquarters' imply about Tom's new sense of himself?

Toolkit

W **Colloquial language**

Strict rules for English are not always applied to informal language. This is called colloquial or vernacular language, meaning it is local to a particular area and is related to the way people speak. Writers often try to capture the particular qualities of spoken language by incorporating it in their dialogue.

- Sometimes people forget (or can't be bothered!) to include all of the verbs that are necessary. A phrase like *You got* is missing the verb 'have'. Find other examples of missing verbs in the extract.

- Short forms are also a characteristic of colloquial language. Some of these, from the text, include: *warn't, ain't, you're, wouldn't*. Which of these are colloquial expressions, and which are more standard English usage?

Should children be allowed to work?

Is it a right for children to work? Or should there be strict laws against it? Much of what we know about the horrors of child labour comes from the reports into the working conditions of children employed in the factories, textile mills and coal mines of Europe in the nineteenth century.

Working children played an important role in the Industrial Revolution, particularly in the United Kingdom, where industrialization was at an advanced stage. Children as young as four years of age went out to work in what were often extremely dangerous and unpleasant working conditions.

Reports into these working conditions led to changes in the legislation (laws).

Report

From the Sadler Committee Report, 1832

In 1832, Michael Sadler, an English reformer, led a parliamentary investigation into the working conditions in the textile factories of England, Scotland and Wales. The immediate effect of the report was the passage of the Factory Act of 1833, making it illegal for children under nine years of age to work in textile factories. Children aged between nine and thirteen were not allowed to work for more than a 48-hour week.

The following account is from one of many interviews undertaken to compile evidence for the report.

✺ Peter Smart, called in and examined ✺

You say you were locked up night and day? — *Yes.*

Do the children ever attempt to run away? — *Very often.*

Were they pursued and brought back again? — *Yes, the overseer pursued them, and brought them back.*

5   Did you ever attempt to run away? — *Yes, I ran away twice.*

And you were brought back? — *Yes, and I was sent up to the master's loft, and thrashed with a whip for running away.*

Were you bound to this man? — *Yes, for six years.*

By whom were you bound? — *My mother got 15s for the six*
10 *years.*

Do you know whether the children were, in point of fact, compelled to work during the whole time they were engaged? — *Yes, they were.*

By law? — *I cannot say by law, but they were compelled by*
15 *the master. I never saw any law used there but the law of their own hands.*

To what mill did you next go? — *To Mr Webster's, at Battus Den, within eleven miles of Dundee.*

In what situation did you act there? — *I acted as overseer.*

20 At 17 years of age? — *Yes.*

Did you inflict the same punishment that you yourself had experienced? — *I went as an overseer; not as a slave, but as a slave-driver.*

What were the hours of labour in that mill? — *My master*
25 *told me that I had to produce a certain quantity of yarn, the hours were at that time fourteen. I said that I was not able to produce the quantity of yarn that was required. I told him if he took the timepiece out of the mill I would produce that quantity, and after that time I found no difficulty in*
30 *producing the quantity.*

How long have you worked per day in order to produce the quantity your master required? — *I have worked for nineteen hours.*

Was this a water-mill? — *Yes, water and steam, both.*

35 To what time have you worked? — *I have seen the mill going till it was past 12 o'clock on the Saturday night.*

So that the mill was still working on the Sabbath morning? — *Yes.*

Were the workmen paid by the piece, or by the day? — *No,*
40 *all had stated wages.*

Wordpool

to pursue (line 3)

to compel (12)

to engage (13)

to inflict (21)

exceedingly (46)

fatigued (46)

Did not that almost compel you to use great severity to the hands then under you? — *Yes, I was compelled often to beat them, in order to get them to attend to their work, from their being over-wrought.*

45 Were not the children exceedingly fatigued at that time? — *Yes, exceedingly fatigued.*

Did you find that the children were unable to pursue their labour properly to that extent? — *Yes, they have been brought to that condition, that I have gone and fetched up*
50 *the doctor to them, to see what was the matter with them, and to know whether they were able to rise or not. We have had great difficulty in getting them up out of bed.*

When that was the case, how long have they been in bed, generally speaking? — *Perhaps not above four or five hours*
55 *in their beds.*

Boys working in a spinning mill, 1910

Comprehension

1 What is 'the law of their own hands'?

2 What is Peter's definition of an overseer's role?

3 What is the significance of the timepiece in Peter's account?

4 What does it mean to be paid by the piece instead of by the day?

5 Why do you think Peter's mother allowed her son to be 'bound'?

Researching a presentation

In some countries, children are forced into labour by their impoverished parents. What effects do you think this has on the children? There are many organizations which work to protect children. Research one such organization and find out what it has achieved.

- Find out about the aims of the organization and when and how it was started.
- Find out how the organization has helped children.
- Give examples of children whose lives have been improved as a result.
- Present your research to your group in a five-minute presentation.

Talking points

1 What do you know about child labour laws in your country?

2 If children are allowed to work, what is being done to limit the hours they work so that their health doesn't suffer and they can attend school?

foot. I lifted my head to call out to Papa to come and see my work – and saw the man in the orange jumpsuit striding towards us.

Mama wailed piteously, then plucked at her hem where she'd hidden the tiny bit of money we had. She knelt in the sand, her arms outstretched, our few coins in her upturned palms. But the man shook his head. He placed his hand on the belt that held his gun.

'Take me,' Papa begged him. 'Spare the woman and the girl.'

Again the man shook his head. Then he reached into his pocket and took out a giant cutting tool. With one mighty snap he severed the links where the fence had been patched. He yanked on the fence so hard it cried out in protest, and peeled it back as if it were made of cloth.

'Hurry,' he said. 'Once the light comes, I will have to go back to patrolling.'

We didn't fully comprehend what he was saying, but we didn't wait.

'You go first,' Papa said to me. 'I want you to be the first in our family to taste freedom.'

I scrambled through the fence, stood next to the man in the orange jumpsuit and looked back at our homeland as the sun began to turn its fields to gold.

'You will miss it for a long time,' the man said to me. 'I still do.'

I stared up at him.

'Yes,' he said. 'I outran the Old Man long ago.' Mama crawled through and kissed the man's boots. He simply helped her to her feet.

'Quickly now,' he said, once Papa had made it through.

'Walk, as fast as you can, until you see a house with white flowers out front. Go round to the back and tell them Robert sent you. They will feed you and hide you until night. Then they will send you to the next safe house, which will send you to the next, and the next – until finally you are in the city and can be swallowed up by all the people there.'

'How do we know we can trust these people?' Mama asked.

'They are our countrymen,' he said. 'You will find many of us here. Now go!'

We did as he instructed, and found the house with the white flowers just as the morning sun broke through the clouds. A woman there brought us inside, gave us water and meat and led us to mats where we could rest. It had been so long since I'd slept on anything other than bare, open ground that I fell asleep at once.

I awoke sometime later and saw that Papa's mat was empty. I stood and wandered outside. The sun was setting, so all I could see was his silhouette against the deepening sky. He raised his arms to the heavens and started to hum. And then I saw Papa dance.

PATRICIA MCCORMICK

Looking closely

1 Explain how the following similes help to create the dramatic atmosphere of the story: a) 'uncoiled, like a snake' b) 'like scorpions looking for a place to dig'.

2 What words and phrases describe Papa's strength?

3 Where had Mama hidden the family's money?

4 When are the girl's own particular skills needed? What can she do, that her parents can't?

5 Select three different emotions experienced by members of the family in the story. Explain what they are and how each is conveyed.

GLOSSARY

A **safe house** is a place where those who are running away from danger can seek refuge.

Comprehension

1 Why did Papa cross the river more than once? What were the dangers?

2 The family intended to dig underneath the fence and crawl through while it was still dark. What hindrances did they face?

3 What did you think was going to happen when the man patrolling the fence approached the family?

4 Why did Mama offer the man in the orange jumpsuit the little bit of money that they had?

5 Why and how did the man in the orange jumpsuit help the family?

Talking points

1 How can dancing celebrate human freedom?

2 What kind of situations are people who use safe houses escaping from?

What is a landscape of toil?

Hard labour is a fact of life for many people who work the land, often struggling to feed themselves and their families. Oppressed people throughout history have suffered under the hands of cruel masters and employers.

Often it is the goods and artefacts left, the old industrial equipment and landscapes, that remind us of the suffering of workers of the past.

Old tobacco scales from
Thrace in Greece

Poem

The following poem, 'Tobaccco Pickers', is by Kocho Racin, who was born in Veles, Macedonia. A writer and a revolutionary, he campaigned for better working conditions for peasants and workers, and worked for a time in his father's ceramics workshop. What is he weighing up in this poem?

∾ Tobacco Pickers ∾

Bronze stones and cold scales:
but they'll never weigh
our tobacco-bane,
our salt sweat.

5 From night-blurred summer daybreaks
to godforsaken winter lightdeaths,
tobacco drinks our pain,
sweat, blood and strength.
Our faces thin, and a bronze weight
10 sits cold on our hearts.

First light, dew-wet, we're there,
bent double in our home-fields,
automatic pickers:
leaf, leaf, pick –
15 leaf, leaf, tie –
leaf, leaf, turn over, push down –
leaf, leaf, thread – patient, sad
on long sweatbead strings.
Rage and hope and hate,
20 milk-blind eyes stare

at leaves, leaves, paper-bronze,
the hard pages of an unlucky life.
Tie, next, tie, next quiet, necessary.
Now you know.

25 It's weigh-up day.
No scales will do it: this bane
pushes on and on into the heart.
Nothing can balance it:
not sadness – but rage:
30 and into our milkblind eyes
its storm wells up.

The scales hold bronze leaves
and in our hearts rage the great storms
of bronze sadness, bronze tobacco,
35 bronze salt sweat from our hands.

KOCHO RACIN

Poem

The poet James Berry was born in Jamaica in 1924, where he spent his childhood before travelling to the United States and later the United Kingdom where he has lived ever since. For Berry, aspects of the landscape of Jamaica will always remind him of the life of toil of previous generations of slave workers.

❧ Old Slave Villages ❧

The windmills are dead
Their tombs are empty towers

Where high estate walls are broken down
Wire fences control the boundaries

5   Thatched slave shacks are gone
In their place – zinc houses, gardens

The great houses, now derelict,
Turned to school grounds – or hotels

The vast fields of sugar cane
10   Are pastures, with cattle grazing

The tombs of landscape windmills
Are broken empty towers.

JAMES BERRY

Toolkit

Hyphens

Hyphens join two words to create one idea. For example, in the poem 'Tobacco Pickers' there are several hyphenated words such as 'dew-wet' that create a new single idea. In this poem there are four more hyphenated words. Identify them and explain what new meaning they create. Then write sentences with at least two of your own hyphenated words.

Women picking tobacco in Jamaica in 1900

Talking points

1   What places do you know of that remind you of past lives of hardship?

2   What do you know about the lives of the people who produce the food and other products you consume?

What is it like to be in hiding?

What would it be like to be in hiding, and in fear of your life if you were discovered? Can you imagine what it would be like to live in a secret room or a crawl space, never to enjoy the freedom of walking around in the open air? What kind of perspective would this give you on the lives of others?

Autobiography

From *Incidents in the Life of a Slave Girl* (1861) by Harriet Jacobs

Harriet Brent Jacobs was a slave for the first 27 years of her life. Born in Edenton, North Carolina, USA, in 1813, Harriet was raised by her freed grandmother. Harriet learned to read, write, and sew under her first mistress, and had hoped to be freed by her. When her mistress died, Harriet was given to Dr James Norcom, who is called Dr Flint in the narrative. Although Dr Flint eventually freed Harriet's children, he was a not a good master to Harriet. Eventually Harriet ran away and hid herself in the crawl space at her grandmother's house. From there, she read, sewed, and watched over her children from a hole in the roof, waiting for an opportunity to escape to the northern states of America, where slavery had been abolished.

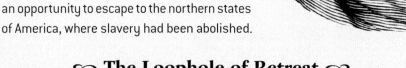

෨ The Loophole of Retreat ෬

A small shed had been added to my grandmother's house years ago. Some boards were laid across the joists at the top, and between these boards and the roof was a very small garret, never occupied by anything but rats and mice. It was
5 a pent roof, covered with nothing but shingles, according to the southern custom for such buildings. The garret was only nine feet long and seven wide. The highest part was three feet high, and sloped down abruptly to the loose board floor. There was no admission for either light or air. My uncle
10 Phillip, who was a carpenter, had very skilfully made a concealed trap-door, which communicated with a storeroom. The storeroom opened upon a piazza.

> **GLOSSARY**
>
> A **pent** roof is an old-fashioned term for a sloping roof.
>
> A **piazza** is a covered room or walkway, like a colonnade on the outside of a building.
>
> A **gimlet** is a tool used for boring holes.

lives – all that was over. As the darkness thickened, the snow flakes grew more abundant and the cold of the air more intense. At last, one by one, swiftly, one after the other, the white peaks of the distant hills vanished into blackness. The
80 breeze rose to a moaning wind. I saw the black central shadow of the eclipse sweeping towards me. In another moment all was rayless obscurity. The sky was absolutely black.

A horror of this great darkness came on me. I was cold to my
85 marrow, and the pain I felt in breathing overcame me. Then in the sky appeared the edge of the sun again as a red-hot arc. I got off my Time Machine to recover myself. As I stood sick and confused, I saw again a thing moving towards the shore. It was a round thing, the size of a football perhaps,
90 and tentacles trailed down from it. It seemed black against the blood-red water and it was hopping fitfully about. I felt I was fainting. A terrible dread of lying helpless in that remote and awful twilight sustained me while I clambered upon the saddle of my Time Machine

95 Then, gentlemen, I returned.

H. G. WELLS

Writing science fiction

W Now it's your turn to create a work of science fiction. Use your imagination to create a utopia or a dystopia.

- Think of a frightening and chilling scenario or a utopian vision. It could be a short story or the introductory chapter to a novel if you prefer.
- Concentrate on your use of descriptive vocabulary and using some really exciting expressions, so that the reader can imagine what it would be like to be there.

to breathe very fast which reminded me of my only experience of mountaineering.

20 Looking round me again, I saw that what I had taken to be a reddish mass of rock was moving slowly towards me. It was a monstrous crab-like creature. Can you imagine a crab as large as that table, with its many legs moving slowly, its big claws swaying, its long antennae waving and feeling, and its
25 eyes on stalks gleaming at you? Its back was covered with ugly lumps and a greenish incrustation. I could see its complicated mouth flickering as it moved.

As I stared at this sinister creature crawling towards me, I felt a tickling on my cheek as though a fly had lighted there.
30 I tried to brush it away with my hand, but in a moment it had returned, and almost immediately came another by my ear. As I tried again to brush it away, I caught something threadlike which was drawn swiftly out of my hand. In fright, I turned and saw that I had grasped the antenna of
35 another monster crab that stood just behind me. Its evil eyes were wriggling on their stalks, its mouth was all alive with appetite, and its vast claws, smeared with an algal slime, were descending upon me.

In a moment my hand was on the lever of my Time Machine,
40 and I had placed a month between myself and these monsters. But I was still on the same beach, and I saw them distinctly; dozens of them were crawling in the sombre light. I cannot convey the sense of abominable desolation that hung over the world. The red eastern sky, the blackness
45 northward, the dead sea, the stony beach crawling with these slow-stirring monsters, the poisonous-looking green of the plants, the thin air that hurt my lungs: all contributed to an appalling effect. I moved on a hundred years, and all was still the same.

50 I then travelled on a thousand years or more, drawn on by the mystery of the earth's fate, watching with a strange fascination the sun grow larger and duller in the westward sky, and the life of the old earth ebb away. At last, more than thirty million years hence, the huge red-hot dome of the sun

GLOSSARY

Antennae are the thin, whiskery feelers, or sensory receptors, on either side of the heads of crustaceans, as here, and of insects and butterflies.

Antennae is an example of a Latin word in current use which has retained its Latin plural. The singular is *antenna*. The Latin plural is always used in scientific contexts. The plural antennas is used colloquially for television antennas, or aerials.

Alien model from 1947

55 had come to obscure nearly a tenth part of the dark sky. Then I stopped once more, for the crawling multitude of crabs had disappeared, and the red beach seemed lifeless. Now it was flecked with white and a bitter cold assailed me as white flakes came eddying down. There were fringes of ice
60 along the sea margin, but the main expanse of that salt ocean, all bloody under the eternal sunset, was still unfrozen.

I looked about me to see if any traces of animal life remained but I saw nothing moving, in earth or sky or sea. The green slime on the rocks alone testified that life was not extinct.
65 Suddenly I noticed that the circular outline of the sun had changed. For a minute perhaps I stared aghast at the blackness that was creeping over the day, and then I realized that an eclipse was beginning. Either the moon or the planet Mercury was passing across the sun's disk. The darkness
70 grew; a cold wind began to blow in gusts, and the white flakes in the air increased in number.

From the edge of the sea came a ripple and whisper. Beyond these lifeless sounds the world was silent. Utterly silent. All the sounds of man – the bleating of sheep, the cries of birds,
75 the hum of insects, the stir that makes the background of our

8 The weather

How does the weather affect our way of life?

In this unit you will:

Experience	Read	Create
• the United Kingdom	• fiction	• journals
• Mongolia	• travel writing	• a poem
• the United States	• a poem	• research into weather
• Bohemia	• an historical account	phenomena
• Turkey		

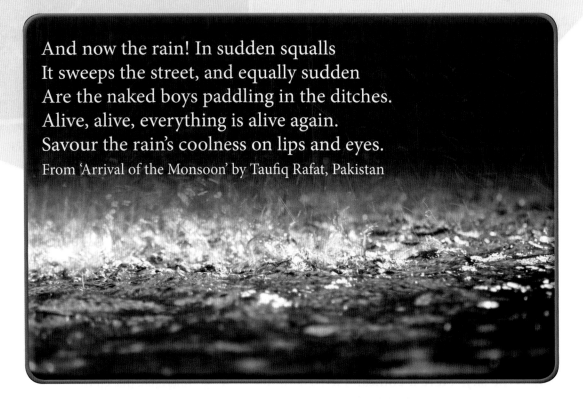

And now the rain! In sudden squalls
It sweeps the street, and equally sudden
Are the naked boys paddling in the ditches.
Alive, alive, everything is alive again.
Savour the rain's coolness on lips and eyes.
From 'Arrival of the Monsoon' by Taufiq Rafat, Pakistan

The seasonal weather patterns of countries differ across the globe and have many different effects on the people living there. For example, in parts of Asia people suffer sweltering heat and long for the monsoon rains to arrive. The poet in the opening quotation describes how life is renewed when the rains finally arrive.

Talking points

1 How many different kinds of weather can you think of which are (a) beneficial and (b) harmful to people?

2 What do you like and dislike about the weather where you are living?

What is extreme weather?

It seems that freak, or extreme, weather is on the increase. In February 2009, London experienced the biggest snowfall in 18 years, bringing the city's transport network to a standstill. In September, a huge outback dust storm swept eastern Australia, turning Sydney into a brilliant orange haze, while many other parts of the state experienced rain, hail, and snow. In October, the Philippines, recovering from devastating floods and landslides, narrowly missed a third typhoon that swept through South-east Asia.

Weather is perhaps never entirely predictable, as the writer Mark Twain suggested in a pretend weather report of a typical New England day in 1876:

'Probably nor'east to sou'west winds, varying to the southard and westward and eastward, and points between: high and low barometer, sweeping round from place to place; probable areas of rain, snow, hail and drought, succeeded or preceded by earthquakes with thunder and lightning.'

Classic fiction

From the *Mill on the Floss* by George Eliot

Flash floods are usually associated with mountainous areas of the world, but they can occur in places where the climate is temperate, such as England. The following extract comes from a classic work of English fiction published in 1860, *The Mill on the Floss*. It was written by George Eliot, the pseudonym for Mary Anne Evans. (Many female writers in the nineteenth century published under male names.)

Maggie is a young woman whose family home is at Dorlcote Mill on the River Floss. As children, she and her younger brother Tom had been extremely close, but just before the time of this extract they had quarrelled. When the River Floss floods, she takes a rowing boat across the flooded fields to try to get to the Mill where she knows her brother and mother are stranded. She is very anxious about them.

ಲ The Flood ಞ

'O God, where am I? Which is the way?' Maggie cried out, in the lonely darkness.

What was happening to them at the Mill? The flood had once nearly destroyed it before. They will be in danger: her
5   mother and her brother, alone there, beyond reach of help! And she imagined the long-loved faces of Tom and her mother looking for help in the darkness – and finding none. She was floating in smooth water now – perhaps far on the flooded fields, straining her eyes against the curtain of gloom
10   that she might catch the first sight of the Mill.

Oh, how welcome was the gradual uplifting of the clouds as objects slowly defined themselves out of the blackness! Yes, she must be out on the fields – those were the tops of hedgerow trees. She knew now that the river lay before her.
15   She seized an oar and began to paddle the boat forward with the energy of hope. Dawn advanced more swiftly: she could soon see the poor cattle crowding on a mound where they had taken refuge. Onward she rowed, driven by the determination to save her brother and mother, her wet

20 clothes clinging round her, and her streaming hair dashed
about by the wind. Maggie was filled also with the strong
love towards her brother that swept away all the recent
quarrels and misunderstandings, and left only the deep,
unshakeable childhood love.

25 'Tom! I'm coming – we will never be separated again!' she
cried out to the shapes of the trees.

Now she recognized a large dark mass in the distance. Ah,
now she knew which way to look for the first glimpse of the
well-known trees and above them the old roof of the mill.

30 She must get her boat into the current of the river, but if she
flowed into it, then she might be carried too far down, and
be unable to guide her boat out of the current again. Visions
of danger began to press upon her, but there was no choice
and she floated into the current. Swiftly she went now,

35 without effort; she began to make out the objects that she
knew more and more clearly in the growing light. These
must be the well-known trees and roofs; she was now not far
off a rushing muddy current that must be the strangely
altered part of the usually gentle river on which the old mill

40 stood. Great God! There were dark objects in it, which might
dash against her boat as she passed, and drown her. What
were those masses? Maggie's heart began to beat in an agony
of dread. Now she must use all her skill to manage the boat
and get out of the current.

45 She could see now that the bridge was broken. Colour was
beginning to awake now, and as she approached the fields,
she could see the trees, but oh, how deep they lay in the
water! And where was the roof of the mill? But the house
stood firm, drowned up to the first storey, but still firm – or

50 was it broken in at the end towards the mill? With joy that
overcame all distress, Maggie neared the front of the house.
At first she heard no sound and saw no object moving. Her
boat was on a level with the up-stairs window. She called out
in a loud, piercing voice.

55 'Tom, where are you? Mother, where are you? It's Maggie!'

Soon, from the window of the attic she heard Tom's voice.

'Who is it? Have you brought a boat?'

'Tom, it's Maggie! Where is Mother?'

60 'She is not here: she's safe with our aunts. I'll come down to the lower window.'

'Are you all alone, Maggie?' said Tom, in a voice of deep astonishment, as he opened the window on a level with the boat.

65 'Yes, Tom: God has taken care of me, to bring me to you. Get in quickly.'

'Give me the oar, Magsie,' said Tom, using the old childhood name as he climbed into the boat.

Maggie could make no answer, feeling only a great happiness. Tom rowed with more vigour than poor Maggie.
70 The boat was soon in the current again, and soon they would be at the village.

Nothing else was said when suddenly a new danger was being carried towards them by the river. Some wooden machinery had just given way on one of the wharves, and
75 huge pieces were being floated along. The sun was rising now, and the wide area of desolation was spread out in dreadful clarity around them – and in dreadful clarity floated onwards the threatening masses.

A large company in a passing boat observed their danger,
80 and shouted, 'Get out of the current!'

But that could not be done at once, and Tom, looking before him as huge fragments, clinging together in fatal fellowship, made one wide mass across the stream.

'It is coming, Maggie!' Tom said, in a deep, hoarse voice,
85 loosing the oars, and clasping her.

The next instant the boat was no longer visible.

But soon the keel of the boat reappeared, a black speck on the golden water.

Looking closely

1 How does the writer's use of punctuation – the question mark, the exclamation mark and the dash – help to convey Maggie's emotions? (paragraphs 1 and 2)

2 Why did Maggie have to row hard at the beginning but, by paragraph 5, travel 'swiftly' and 'without effort'?

3 What does the word 'unshakeable' tell you about Maggie's feelings for her brother?

4 Describe the range of Maggie's emotions in paragraph 5. What has become apparent, that turns Maggie into 'an agony of dread'?

5 How can you tell that Tom has forgotten his quarrel with Maggie?

GLOSSARY

Wharves (the plural of *wharf*) are wooden structures built along the river bank to enable boats to moor, load and unload.

90 The boat reappeared, but brother and sister had gone down in an embrace never to be parted, living through again in one supreme moment the days when they had clasped their little hands in love, and roamed the daisied fields together.

EPILOGUE:
Nature repairs her ravages – repairs them with her sunshine,
95 and with human labour. The desolation wrought by that flood had left little visible trace on the face of the earth, five years after. The fifth autumn was rich in golden cornstacks, rising in thick clusters among the distant hedgerows. The wharves and warehouses on the Floss were busy again, with
100 echoes of eager voices.

But all is not as before. The uptorn trees are not rooted again, and the parted hills are left scarred. If there is a new growth, the trees are not the same as the old, and the hills underneath their green verdure bear scars. To the eyes that
105 have dwelt on the past, there is no thorough repair.

GEORGE ELIOT

Toolkit

Conjunctions

Often people are told that it is wrong to start a sentence with a conjunction like 'and' or 'but'. However, many sentences start with conjunctions. Writers like to use them to create a particular effect. There are several instances of this in *The Flood*, including:

But soon the keel of the boat reappeared, a black speck on the golden water.

Find the other examples in *The Flood* and explain what effect the author has created in each case. **W**

Comprehension

1 At what point in the extract does the full extent of the flood damage become apparent?

2 How is Maggie's cry in paragraph 4 a forewarning of what is about to happen?

3 What do the 'dark objects' and the 'fatal fellowship' of the huge fragments mean to Maggie and Tom?

4 What does the image of 'roamed daisied fields together' symbolize? In what way is this a positive ending to the tragedy? (line 92)

5 What ravages are repaired, and what scars remain at the end of the dramatic conclusion to the novel?

Journal

What is the most extreme weather you have experienced? Describe how you felt and whether you were in danger.

Travel writing

From *Letters from Tsengel, Mongolia* 1998, by Louisa Waugh

Map showing the Altai Mountains in Mongolia

After spending two years working in Ulaanbaatar, the capital of Mongolia, Louisa Waugh moved into a remote village in the Altai Mountains in the far north-west of the country on its border with Siberia in Russia. She spent a year in the remote community of Tsengel from where she sent monthly newsletters to a British journal. Here she describes a winter morning in 1998.

೫ A Frozen World ೫

I wake up and my world has frozen. Everything, and I mean everything – my water, tomato paste, soap – is encased in thick, milky ice. I light a candle, stand up in my sleeping bag and pull on another layer of clothing. Shivering, I take a
5 knife to the water bucket and hack at the ice until bubbles rise to the surface. Lighting my small stove is difficult because the wood, which was damp, is now frozen. By the time my smoky fire is finally crackling and heating the water and ice in the kettle, the outside temperature has risen to
10 -25°C. I've never been so cold in my life. I know the mountains surrounding my village will be covered in fresh snow but I can't see anything because my window is coated with thick ice. On this dark, freezing winter morning, venturing to the communal outside toilet is quite an
15 endurance test. But, after two cups of steaming black coffee I

Wordpool

communal [line 14]

endurance [15]

concealed [21]

herder [29]

settlement [29]

ricochet [44]

livestock [54]

am wrapped up and off to work, just as the sky is gradually brightening.

My school is a ten-minute walk alongside the Hovd river which flows through the village. The river has now frozen so
20 solid that horses are being ridden and cars driven over it. Everything but my eyes is concealed from the freezing air and my gloved fingers are pushed down into my pockets.

'Off to work, Louisa?' calls my neighbour, Sansar-Huu. 'Don't worry, it's quite warm today – just wait till it gets
25 really cold!'

Our school has no electricity or running water, but each small classroom is heated by a wood-burning stove. This morning we all wear our coats during lessons. Wind-burned children from herders' settlements outside the village board
30 at the school, twelve to a dormitory. Their parents pay the fees in meat and wood. At break we jostle to be near the staff-room stove and my colleagues pull their fur hats back on.

'You sit by the fire, Louisa – you must be freezing,' offers
35 Gansukh, my fellow English teacher.

After our classes, Gansukh and I cross the street to the post office, which is crowded, as the weekly post has arrived. Clutching two letters, I walk home with Gansukh and a couple of our students, passing herders trading camel, sheep,
40 goat and wolf skins. We stop *en route* for bowls of tea at a friend's house.

At home, I need more water. I lift the creaking lid of the well opposite our yard, but the water is frozen so hard that I can hear the rocks I fling down the shaft ricochet off the ice.
45 Taking the axe, I set out for the nearby river to make my own well.

That afternoon it snows heavily as Sansar-Huu and I saw logs in the yard. 'How long will it be this cold?' I ask him as I stand panting, my face flushed and numb.
50 'Oh, it gets as low as -48°C degrees here,' he tells me, grinning. 'But we need this snowy winter. Even by October

---

GLOSSARY

-25˚C is minus 25 degrees Centigrade, or Celsius. This is equivalent to -13˚**F** (minus 13 degrees Fahrenheit).

-48˚C is -54˚F.

En route is a French expression used in English. It means 'on the way'.

How do we describe the weather?

Many people throughout the centuries have come up with intriguing explanations and descriptions for unusual weather conditions. Have you ever gazed in wonder at the observable phenomena of the sky, and the effects of precipitation (rain, snow, dew, etc.)?

Have you ever seen an aurora, or a fog so dense that you could get lost in it?

Poem

In the very short poem 'Fog', the American poet Carl Sandburg personifies the fog. This means that he describes the fog as a living creature.

ℰ Fog ℛ

The fog comes
On little cat feet

It sits looking
Over harbor and city
5   On silent haunches
And then moves on.

CARL SANDBURG

Writing about phenomena

Now it's your turn! Write your own poem or a description in which you compare an observable natural phenomenon with a living creature. This could be a person or an animal.

- Think about your personification and how you can sustain it. This means you extend your idea as Carl Sandburg did. His fog had 'little cat feet' and 'haunches' and moved like a cat.
- Make a list of your points of comparison before you start.
- Make each word and phrase contribute to the general idea. Make it short, but powerful!

Toolkit

An extended metaphor is a metaphor that compares how something is similar to something else in lots of ways.

The poem 'Fog' is an extended metaphor. What are all the ways fog is compared to a cat?

My heart leaps up when I behold
A rainbow in the sky.

WILLIAM WORDSWORTH

rainbow, *n.*

1. a. An arc of spectral colours, usually identified as red, orange, yellow, green, blue, indigo, and violet, that appears in the sky opposite the sun as a result of the refractive dispersion of sunlight in drops of rain or mist.

Writing a description

W Think of a phenomenon to do with the atmosphere. It could be a type of storm, a rainbow or other halo effect, or some unusual cloud formation that you have seen.

- Find examples of poetic description.
- Research a scientific explanation.
- Describe the phenomenon in your own words, as you experienced it.

Make use of all the information available to you to inform your personal account.

An historical account

The following account of the northern lights was written in Bohemia in 1570. Bohemia is in Central Europe, and is now part of the Czech Republic. When this account was written, people didn't understand that auroras (polar lights) were a natural phenomenon, caused by magnetic storms in the Earth's upper atmosphere.

What does this account reveal about the fears and beliefs of those who observed the astonishing effects?.

Talking points

When did you last experience some unusual and dramatic effects of the weather? How did it affect you?

✑ An Uncommon Omen ✑

An uncommon omen was observed among the clouds over Bohemia on the 12th January, 1570. it lasted four hours. First, a black cloud like a great mountain appeared where several stars had been shining. Above the cloud there was a bright strip of light as of burning sulphur and in the shape of a ship. From this arose many burning torches, almost like candles, and between these, two great pillars, one to the east and one to the north. Fire coursed down the pillars like drops of blood, and the town was illuminated as if it were on fire. The watchmen sounded the alarm and woke the inhabitants so they could witness this miraculous sign from God. All were dismayed and said that never within the memory of man had they seen or heard tell of such a sinister sight.

Two views of the aurora borealis (northern lights)

Extension reading

From *Against the Storm* by Gaye Hiçyılmaz

The following extract comes from a story set in Turkey. Mehmet has moved with his family from the country to the city of Ankara in search of a better life. But life is hard for the family, who have to live in a shanty town outside the city. Mehmet makes a friend called Muhlis, and they are occasionally employed by Zekiye Hanim to work in her garden. They go to her house by cart pulled by Yildiz, Muhlis's horse. On this occasion, the weather has been getting increasingly hot, and a storm is threatening.

Mehmet lived in a shanty town like this one

> **GLOSSARY**
>
> **Hanim**, as in Zekiye Hanim, means 'Mrs' or 'Miss'.
>
> **Yildiz**, the name of the horse, means 'star'.
>
> **Korsan** is the name of Mehmet's dog.

> **Wordpool**
>
> to be plagued with [line 3]
>
> scythe [17]
>
> oppressive [19]
>
> flurry [19]
>
> cone [62]
>
> crimson [114]
>
> veined [124]

ഔ The storm ൭

It was hotter still. Mehmet's mother had nailed sheets over most of the empty windows but it was impossible to keep the house cool. By day they were plagued with flies. They settled on your food as you raised the spoon to your mouth and
5 they crawled along your eyelids and round your nose. With the coming of darkness, the mosquitoes rose up in great, humming clouds. Even when you thought you had covered yourself completely with a sheet, the high whine of yet another disturbed your sleep. The children scratched and
10 scratched until they bled. Tonight it was extra bad. The older people said that there was a storm coming: flies always came

indoors before a storm. Once Mehmet awoke and he sat with his grandfather and they watched the lightning forking in the distance, but no rain fell. In
15 the morning he was to go to Zekiye Hanim's house, so Mehmet was glad to get up early. He sharpened the scythe, and then hurried out on hearing the clink of Yildiz's hooves. It was oppressively hot. A sudden flurry blew the dust
20 up into their faces. The wind was warm and the grit grated between their teeth. They urged Yildiz on, eager to reach the cooling green of the walled garden.

A scythe leaning up against a wood-shed

They set to work, Mehmet scything the grass and Muhlis
25 weeding between the rose bushes. It was too hot to talk and the garden was quieter than they had ever known it. Not a leaf stirred. The cut grass shrivelled as soon as it fell. Zekiye Hanim, who liked to talk and help a little, sat on the balcony and fanned herself and looked out to the distant mountains.
30 She said that a storm must come. At lunch-time they knocked on the door and fetched their tray of bread, olives and fruit and searched for the shade. Today the shadows were warm. They soaked their heads and shirts with water from the hose, trying to refresh themselves, but their clothes felt heavy and
35 chill instead. After lunch they raked the grass into a pile and then they began sweeping and washing the paths and steps. Suddenly Zekiye Hanim banged on the window and shook her head, as if she did not want them to continue working. She pointed repeatedly to something in the distance and
40 when they did not understand she came back on to the balcony.

'Your work will be wasted. Look over there: don't you see the storm coming?'

'I don't see any clouds,' said Mehmet, 'really I don't. Let us
45 tidy up for you.'

'Some storms come without clouds. If you know the signs you can tell. Look!'

'I can't see anything,' said Mehmet. 'It looks to me like the sun is shining on the mountains.'

50 'Look more carefully.'

'I can see a brightness and the mountains have a dark line around them.' Then he shivered: a sharp, twirling wind went over the garden and up the street. They heard windows bang and the scratch of dry papers blown along the base of the
55 wall. He shivered again and Korsan ran up to him with his tail between his legs and whined.

'Now,' insisted Zekiye Hanim, 'look again. I've known it was coming for a long time, though I hoped that it would not.'

'Do you see that?' called Muhlis. The light behind the
60 mountains – a strange greenish-yellow light – became brighter and there, far beyond the other side of the great city were three cones of darkness, which looked as though a giant hand had scribbled them in the sky. As they watched, the cones grew in size.

65 'Is it smoke?' Mehmet wondered if something very big was burning.

'No, it's the wind ... '

'But you can't see the wind ... '

'It's the dirt and dust caught up in the wind. In about half an
70 hour it will be here. It'll be a very strong wind.'

'Strong enough to blow things down?' Mehmet thought anxiously of his family in that half-finished building. Another gust rustled the leaves in the garden.

'It'll be strong enough to blow a few roofs off. Now, do you
75 still want to help me?'

They nodded. 'Then take your shoes off and come indoors quickly and help me fasten down all the shutters and windows before that wind reaches us.' They dropped their tools hastily and entered the house for the first time.

80 Mehmet had seen a few films on neighbours' televisions and
so he knew that people in foreign lands lived like this with
bathrooms and polished wooden floors and bedrooms where
children slept all alone, except for hundreds of toys. He had
never thought that just one hour's walk away from where he
85 lived there could be houses like this. In the village there had
been richer and poorer families too, but they had all lived in
much the same way. Now he had stepped into a different
world. He saw a whole shelf of different coloured towels in
the bathroom and a row of dresses hanging up in a
90 cupboard: a whole row, like you could see in a shop.
Everywhere there were objects, pictures, curtains, rugs —
things that were just there because they looked pretty.

The sky was darkening rapidly and it was not with the
coming of evening. The yellow light was deepening and the
95 brightness fading. They quickly started untying the cushions
from the white chairs, and began to pack away the furniture
on the balcony. Another strong gust thrust against the
balcony doors as they tried to shut them. From somewhere
up the street they heard glass breaking. Outside, the roses
100 glowed very clearly in the lightless garden.

'You had better get that grass into the sacks before the wind
really comes,' she reminded them and they ran barefoot into
the garden. They saw papers swept high up and spinning
around in the air, high above the trees. The heap of grass
105 lifted and began to fan upwards. Muhlis leapt forward with
his arms outstretched to try and save it. He seemed to
stumble. He did not cry out. They heard a gasping sound as
though the wind had torn his words from him. Then he
curled up on the ground with his hands around his foot. He
110 had trodden heavily on to the curved blade of the scythe that
Mehmet had hastily flung down amongst the grass cuttings.
There was blood everywhere. Mehmet tried to make him
take his hand away and then the wound opened like a
crimson mouth. Mehmet was frightened of the blood: if he
115 could wash it away, perhaps the cut was not so bad. He
grabbed the hose and directed the jet of cold, clear water on
to Muhlis's foot. It kept on bleeding. Muhlis lay very still
with his face the colour of dust and his other hand pressed to

his mouth. The old lady begged them to go to a hospital. She
120 would pay, she pleaded, but Muhlis refused. He crawled on
to the marble steps while the wind rose higher and higher.
Mehmet, with a shaking hand, poured iodine into the cut
and Muhlis lay back with his cheek on the white and gold
veined marble. Zekiye Hanim knelt down and bandaged the
125 wound herself and Mehmet saw that she was crying. The
blood soaked through the bandage and she begged them
again to let her go for help but Muhlis refused and leaning
on Mehmet, dragged himself down the steps and on to the
cart.

130 'It was my fault,' said Mehmet, picking up the reins. He had
thrown down the scythe: everybody knows that you should
stand a scythe up. Then at least you can see the blade before
it cuts you. He remembered that the scythe was still there,
lying like a scorpion in the grass. He jumped down and
135 pulled it clear and hung it up on a branch so that the blade
swung to and fro amongst the rose blooms. Well, it could
just stay there, it and the other tools; they could stay there
and perhaps the coming rain would wash their blades clean.

'It wasn't your fault,' Muhlis muttered as Mehmet climbed
140 back on to the cart. 'Things happen like that.'

GAYE HIÇYILMAZ

Comprehension

1 What signs are there of the approaching storm?

2 What details tell you that it was very hot?

3 What are Mehmet's reactions to the interior of Zekiye Hanim's house ?

4 How do the similes 'like a crimson mouth' (line 114) and 'like a scorpion in the grass' (line 134) add to your understanding of the scene?

5 Explain how the accident happened.

9 Cities

Oh Samarkand! Where is Samarkand?

In this unit you will:

Experience
- Samarkand
- London
- Paris
- Istanbul
- Venice
- Delhi

Read
- a poem
- fiction
- autobiography
- non-fiction

Create
- data analysis
- historical analysis
- a description
- an opening scene
- journal entries

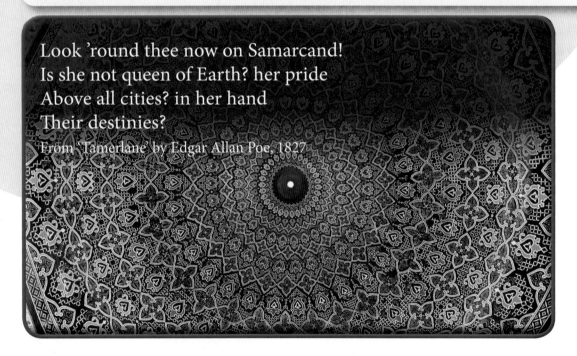

Look 'round thee now on Samarcand!
Is she not queen of Earth? her pride
Above all cities? in her hand
Their destinies?
From 'Tamerlane' by Edgar Allan Poe, 1827

Do you know where Samarkand is? One of the oldest cities in the world, it was once part of Persia and is now in Uzbekistan. In its heyday, up to the fourteenth century, when it was ruled by Tamerlane, it was a major city on the old Silk Road – the trade route between China and Western Europe that runs all the way to the Mediterranean Sea.

Why do you think writers continue to imagine the delights of Samarkand? What does it represent in people's imagination?

What are the top ten cities?

Which do you think are the ten biggest cities in the world at the present time in terms of population? Make a list of them. If you had made your top ten list in 1950, probably around the time when your grandparents were children, do you think your list would have been the same? Can you think of any ways in which your 1950 list would have been different? What do you think are the reasons for the changes? When you have finished your discussion, compare your top tens with the ones on page 151.

What's so special about towns and cities?

Poets and writers often dwell on the lost cities and empires of the ancient world. Sometimes these exotic places are bigger in the imagination than they could ever have been in reality.

In 'Town', the English writer Holbrook Jackson is making a general point rather than writing about a specific town, city, race or nation. Below is an extract from his poem, first published in 1913.

෨ Town ෬

I write of Town, not of this town or that town,
not of London or Paris, neither of Venice nor
Oxford, nor Florence, nor Bath, nor Bruges, nor
Rome; nor yet write I of Bagdad or Babylon,
Damascus or Samarkand: good towns all, but
5 I write not of them. I write of Town. I celebrate
all of these master cities domed or towered or
turreted, roofed in red or grey or purple, walled
or free, filled with trees or threaded by river
or canal, piercing heaven with spire or
10 striking it with minaret, it is all of these in the
final expression of man's creativeness – Town.

Holbrook Jackson

Talking points

1 What is your idea of an ideal town or city?

2 What would be the opposite?

3 Do you know of any cities that followed a 'master plan'?

A nineteenth-century view of Florence by the English artist John Brett.

Why do more people live in cities today?

A recent report by the United Nations established that for the first time in history more people live in cities than in small towns and rural communities. This has important consequences for all aspects of our lives, from the way we produce our food to the quality of the air we breathe and the kind of work we do.

- Do you recognize any of these cities? What features or landmarks helped you to identify each one?

Teheran

Hong Kong

London

Cape Town

Istanbul

New York

Forbidden City, Beijing

Paris

Why do populations in cities continue to increase?

The 10 largest cities today	
1 Tokyo, Japan	28,025,000 people
2 Mexico City, Mexico	18,131,000
3 Mumbai, India	18,042,000
4 São Paulo, Brazil	17,711,000
5 New York City, USA	16,626,000
6 Shanghai, China	14,173,000
7 Lagos, Nigeria	13,488,000
8 Los Angeles, USA	13,129,000
9 Calcutta, India	12,900,000
10 Buenos Aires, Argentina	12,431,000

The 10 largest cities in 1500	
1 Beijing, China	672,000
2 Vijayanagar, India	500,000
3 Cairo, Egypt	400,000
4 Hangzhou, China	250,000
5 Tabriz, Iran	250,000
6 Constantinople (Istanbul), Turkey	200,000
7 Gaur, India	200,000
8 Paris, France	185,000
9 Guangzhou, China	150,000
10 Nanjing, China	147,000

The 10 largest cities in 1950	
1 New York, USA	12,463,000
2 London, UK	8,860,000
3 Tokyo, Japan	7,000,000
4 Paris, France	5,900,000
5 Shanghai, China	5,406,000
6 Moscow, Russia	5,100,000
7 Buenos Aires, Argentina	5,000,000
8 Chicago, USA	4,906,000
9 Ruhr, Germany	4,900,000
10 Calcutta, India	4,800,000

The 10 largest cities in 1000	
1 Cordova, Spain	450,000
2 Kaifeng, China	500,000
3 Constantinople (Istanbul), Turkey	400,000
4 Angkor, Cambodia	250,000
5 Kyoto, Japan	175,000
6 Cairo, Egypt	135,000
7 Baghdad, Iraq	125,000
8 Nishapur (Neyshabur), Iran	125,000
9 Al-Hasa, Saudi Arabia	110,000
10 Patan (Anhilwara), India	100,000

Analysing the data

W Read the population charts above. Are there any surprises?

Write a paragraph for each of the questions below.

- What do the charts tell you about the world since 1950?
- What happens when we go back to earlier centuries?
- What is the effect of the growth of megacities? These are cities of more then 10 million people.

Talking points

1 Can you place these cities on a world map?
2 What do these charts tell you about our changing world?

151

Fiction

From *Smith* by Leon Garfield

Crimes committed on city streets today may be different from those of the past, but pick-pockets have long operated in all big cities all over the world, and still do.

This story is about Smith, a poor boy in nineteenth-century London who makes a living by picking people's pockets – that means he is a thief. In Smith's time London was the biggest city in the world and the streets were full of opportunities. Smith's life was like Oliver's in Charles Dickens's great novel *Oliver Twist*.

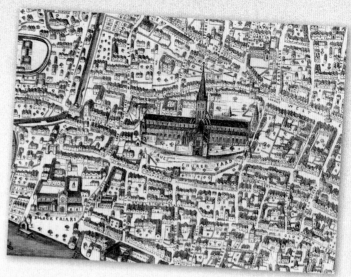

An image of central London from the sixteenth century, showing old St Paul's

๑๐ Smith ๑๕

Smith had a turn of speed that was remarkable, and a neatness in nipping down an alley or vanishing in a court that had to be seen to be believed. Not that it was often seen, for Smith inhabited the tumbledown mazes about St Paul's like
5   the air itself. A rat was like a snail beside Smith, and the most his thousand victims ever got of him was the powerful whiff of his passing and a cold draught in their dexterously emptied pockets.

Only the birds that perched on the church's dome ever saw
10   Smith's entire progress, and as their beady eyes followed him, they chattered savagely, 'Pick-pocket! Pick-pocket! Jug him! Jug-jug-jug him!' His favourite spot was Ludgate Hill, where the world's coaches and carriages met from morning to night, in a horrible confusion. And here, in one or other of
15   the ancient doorways, Smith leaned and grinned while the shouting and cursing and scraping and raging went endlessly, hopelessly on – till, sooner or later, something prosperous would come his way.

At about half past ten of a cold December morning an old
20   gentleman got furiously out of his carriage, in which he'd been trapped for an hour, shook his red fist at his helpless coachman and the roaring but motionless world, and began to stump up Ludgate Hill.

GLOSSARY

Jug is nineteenth-century slang for 'prison'.

Gentlemen, that is gentry or upper-class men, often wore wigs at this time.

A **clerk** is an office worker, generally employed to do paperwork – to write letters and maintain account books, etc.

A **yard** is 36 inches or 90 centimetres.

Word origins

dexterous, also spelt 'dextrous', means having good mental or manual skills. It comes from the Latin word *dexter* meaning 'right-handed'. Left-handed in Latin is sinister, and has negative connotations.

'Pick-pocket! Pick-pocket!' shrieked the cathedral birds in a
25 fury.

He was a country gentleman, judging by his complexion, his
clean old-fashioned coat and his broad-legged, lumbering
walk which bumped out his pockets in a manner most
provoking.

30 Smith twitched his nose and nipped neatly along like a
shadow ...

The old man's pace was variable: sometimes it was brisk,
then he'd slow down, hesitate, look about him as if the
Town had changed much since last he'd visited and he was
35 now no longer confident of his way. He took one turning,
then another; stopped, scratched the crisp edge of his wig,
then eyed the sallow city gentry as if to ask the way, till he
spied another turn, nodded, briskly took it – and came
straight back to Ludgate Hill ...

40 A dingy fellow creaked out of a doorway and made to accost
the old man: but did not. He'd glimpsed Smith. Looks had
been exchanged, shoulders shrugged – and the old villain
gave way to the young one.

On went the old gentleman, confident now in his bearings,
45 deeper and deeper into the forest of the Town where Smith
hunted best.

Now a sharpish wind sprang up, and the cathedral birds
eyed the leaden sky and screeched.

'Pick-pocket! Pick-pocket! Jug-jug-jug him!'

50 The old gentleman was very deep in Smith's country now,
and paused many a time to peer down the lanes and alleys.
Then he'd shake his head vaguely and touch at his coat
pocket – as if a deep sense had warned him of a pair of sharp
eyes fairly cutting into the cloth like scissors. At last he saw
55 something familiar – some landmark he'd remembered –
Godliman Street. Yes: he was in Godliman Street ...

As suddenly as it had sprung up, the wind died – and the
cathedral birds flew back to their dome.

Wordpool

court (line 2)

maze (4)

dingy (40)

to accost (40)

leaden (48)

urchin (80)

speck (83)

Looking closely

1   Why does Smith leave
behind nothing but a
'powerful whiff' and a 'cold
draught'? (lines 6–7)
What do these phrases
describe?

2   What do the words
'shouting and cursing and
scraping and raging' add to
your understanding of the
street scene? Why do you
think the writer used four
words in a row rather than
just one? (line 16)

3   What does it mean that the
gentleman's walk 'bumped
out' his pockets? Why did
Smith find this
'provoking'? (lines 28–9)

4   The old gentleman
'stumped' along the
streets. Why does the
writer choose this verb
rather than 'walked'?

Autobiography

From *Down and Out in Paris and London* by George Orwell

Paris and London have often featured in great novels of the nineteenth and twentieth centuries. In this semi-autobiographical account by the young writer George Orwell, first published in 1933, he describes city life from the point of view of its poorest inhabitants. It starts out with a description of life in a boarding house in Paris.

Street scene in Paris, painted in 1926 by Christopher Wood

ꙮ The rue du Coq'Or, Paris ꙮ

The rue du Coq d'Or, Paris, seven in the morning. A succession of furious, choking yells from the street. Madame Monce, who kept the little hotel opposite mine, had come out on to the pavement to address a lodger on the third floor.
5 Her bare feet were stuck into sabots and her grey hair was streaming down.

Madame Monce: 'How many times have I told you not to squash bugs on the wallpaper? Do you think you've bought the hotel, eh? Why can't you throw them out of the window like everyone else?' The woman on the third floor: '*Vache!*'

10

Thereupon a chorus of yells, as windows were flung open on every side and half the street joined in the quarrel. They shut up abruptly ten minutes later, when a squadron of cavalry rode past and people stopped shouting to look at them.

15

I sketch this scene, just to convey something of the spirit of the rue du Coq d'Or. Not that quarrels were the only thing that happened there – but still, we seldom got through the morning without at least one outburst of this description. Quarrels, and the desolate cries of street hawkers, and the

20

shouts of children chasing orange-peel over the cobbles, and at night loud singing and the sour reek of the refuse-carts, made up the atmosphere of the street.

It was a very narrow street – a ravine of tall, leprous houses, lurching towards one another in queer attitudes, as though

25

they had all been frozen in the act of collapse. All the houses were hotels and packed to the tiles with lodgers, mostly Poles, Arabs and Italians. At the foot of the hotels were tiny bistros.

On Saturday nights there was fighting, and the navvies who

30

lived in the cheapest hotels used to conduct mysterious feuds, and fight them out with chairs and occasionally revolvers. At night the policemen would only come through the street two together. It was a fairly rackety place. And yet amid the noise and dirt lived the usual respectable French shopkeepers,

35

bakers and laundresses and the like, keeping themselves to themselves and quietly piling up small fortunes. It was quite a representative Paris slum.

GEORGE ORWELL

Looking closely

1 What does being 'Down and Out' mean, do you think?

2 Orwell described the buildings as 'leprous', 'lurching' and 'rackety'. What do these words mean, and which ones could also be used to describe a person?

3 List all the sounds Orwell describes that build up a picture of a very noisy neighbourhood.

4 List all the descriptions of rubbish and dirt.

Comprehension

1 How do we know that this is a very crowded part of Paris?

2 Why do you think the people who live here quarrel so much?

3 Why do you think the police liked to patrol this part of the city in groups of two?

4 What do the 'respectable' people who live here do?

Fiction

From *The White Tiger* by Aravind Adiga

This extract from the novel *The White Tiger* by Aravind Adiga is written from the point of view of the driver and servant, Balram Halwai, who works for Mr Ashok. Mr Ashok is a wealthy landowner, whose estates are close to the village where Balram grew up. Both of their lives change dramatically when they move to the city. While they are driving through New Delhi, on the road to the satellite city of Gurgaon, Balram describes his frustration at being caught in a traffic jam.

An autorickshaw and other vehicles waiting at the traffic lights, New Delhi

❧ Traffic Jam in New Delhi ☙

There was a fierce jam on the road to Gurgaon. Every five minutes the traffic would tremble – we'd move a foot – hope would rise – then the red lights would flash on the cars ahead of me, and we'd be stuck again. Everyone honked every now and then, the various horns, each with its own pitch, blended into one continuous wail that sounded like a calf taken from its mother. Fumes filled the air. Wisps of blue exhaust glowed in front of every headlight; the exhaust grew so fat and thick it could not rise or escape, but spread horizontally, sluggish and glossy, making a kind of fog around us. Matches were continually being struck – the drivers of auto-rickshaws lit cigarettes, adding tobacco pollution to petrol pollution.

A man driving a buffalo cart had stopped in front of us; a pile of empty car engine oil cans fifteen feet high had been tied by rope to his cart. His poor water buffalo! To carry all that load – while sucking in this air!

The auto-rickshaw driver next to me began to cough violently – he turned to the side and spat, three times in a row. Some of the spit flecked the side of the Honda City. I glared – I raised my fist. He cringed, and *namasted* me in apology.

'It's like we're in a concert of spitting!' Mr Ashok said, looking at the auto-rickshaw driver.

5

10

15

20

Word origins

Namaste comes from the Sanskrit words *namas* and *te* (to you) and means 'I bow to you'. It is a formal greeting and a show of respect common in South India and is often accompanied by a slight bow made with hands pressed together.

Wordpool

sluggish (line 9)

to cringe (20)

multitudes (31)

to squat (31)

to unfurl (33)

gruel (41)

25 *Well, if you were out there breathing that acid air, you'd be spitting like him too,* I thought.

The cars moved again – we gained three feet – then the red lights flashed and everything stopped again.

Dim streetlights were glowing down onto the pavement on
30 either side of the traffic; and in that orange-hued half light, I could see multitudes of small, thin, grimy people squatting, waiting for a bus to take them somewhere, or with nowhere to go and about to unfurl a mattress and sleep right there. These poor creatures had come from the Darkness to Delhi
35 to find some light – but they were still in the darkness. Hundreds of them, there seemed to be, on either side of the traffic, and their life was entirely unaffected by the jam. Were they even aware that there was a jam? We were like two separate cities – inside and outside the dark egg. I knew I was
40 in the right city. But my father, if he were alive, would be sitting on that pavement, cooking some rice gruel for dinner, and getting ready to lie down and sleep under a streetlamp and I couldn't stop thinking of that and recognizing his features in some beggar out there. So I was in some way out
45 of the car too, even while I was driving it.

ARAVIND ADIGA

Describing the city

Write a description of a part of a town or city that you are familiar with. Perhaps it is where you live or somewhere you visit regularly.

- Decide on what point of view you are going to have. How do you travel there? Are you a visitor or do you live there?
- Be opinionated! What fascinates you about it? Describe the scene and the things that go on there.

Comprehension

1 What kinds of vehicles are caught up in the traffic jam?

2 Who is not affected by the traffic jam?

3 What word does the writer use as a metaphor for the car?

4 Who is in darkness, and who is in light? Where does the writer see himself?

Toolkit

Commas

The rules around commas change over time and their use is debated. You can see a vast number of commas used in 'Traffic Jam in New Delhi'. Each comma is used to separate each additional piece of information. Writers must use their judgment to determine when too much information makes a sentence awkward and confusing rather than graceful and informative. One clear use of a comma is to separate information that tells more about a noun. For example, 'My friend, a registered nurse, gives me great advice about nutrition.' Write five sentences that follow this sentence structure. **W**

When is a city like a work of art?

Do you sometimes think of pictures when you walk through an old city? Do you find yourself comparing what you see with a postcard, a painting, or an old photograph? Perhaps you also remember a scene from a favourite film.

In the following extracts, the writers focus on ways of looking at their favourite cities that relate to art.

Autobiography

From *Istanbul: Memories of a City* by Orhan Pamuk

The writer Orhan Pamuk has lived all his life in Istanbul and has a great affection for the city, and the memories of his childhood there. In the following extract he makes the connection between his fascination for old black-and-white prints and photographs of the city and his love of black and white.

Istanbul's grand past as the centre of the Ottoman Empire can be seen in the grand old buildings that are now in a state of neglect and disrepair. He calls his family home a 'museum house' because of the large formal sitting room where he was not allowed to play. In this room, the curtains were permanently drawn in order to protect the old photographs and objects from the heat, light and dust.

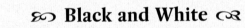

༄ Black and White ༄

Accustomed as I was to the semi-darkness of our bleak museum house, I preferred being indoors. The street below, the avenues beyond, the city's poor neighbourhoods seemed as dangerous as those in a black-and-white gangster film.
5 And with this attraction to the shadow world, I have always preferred the winter to the summer in Istanbul. I love the early evenings when autumn is slipping into winter, when the leafless trees are trembling in the north wind and people in black coats and jackets are rushing home through the
10 darkening streets. I love the overwhelming melancholy when I look at the walls of old apartment buildings and the dark surfaces of neglected, unpainted, fallen-down wooden mansions: only in Istanbul have I seen this texture, this shading. When I watch the black-and-white crowds rushing
15 through the darkening streets on a winter evening, I feel a deep sense of fellowship, almost as if the night has cloaked

Istanbul, Old Town

Word origins

gangster is an American-English term for a criminal. It comes from the Old English word *gang*, meaning 'a going' or passage-way, and *gangr* in Old Norse referring to a group of men.

melancholy is a term for black thoughts, associated with depression and gloom. The ancient Greek word *melankholia* literally means 'black bile', a body fluid, with the connotation of physical illness.

160

our lives, our streets, our every belonging in a blanket of darkness, as if once we're safe in our houses, our bedrooms, our beds, we can return to dreams of our long-gone riches,
20 our legendary past.

The wooden mansions of my childhood, and the smaller, more modest wooden houses in the city's back streets, were in a mesmerising state of ruin. Poverty and neglect had ensured these houses were never painted, and the
25 combination of age, dirt and humidity slowly darkened the wood to give that special colour, that unique texture, so prevalent in the back-street neighbourhood I saw as a child that I took the blackness to be original. Some houses had a brown under-tone, and perhaps there were those in the
30 poorest streets that had never known paint.

In the summer, when these old wooden houses would dry out, turn a dark, chalky, tinderbox brown, you could imagine them catching fire at any moment. During the winter's long cold spells, the snow and the rain endowed these same
35 houses with the mildew hint of rotting wood. So it was too with the old wooden dervish lodges, now mostly abandoned and of interest only to street urchins, ghosts and antique hunters. They would awaken in me the same degrees of fear, worry and curiosity; as I peered at them over the half-broken
40 walls through the damp trees and into the broken windows, a chill would pass through me.

ORHAN PAMUK

GLOSSARY

A **dervish** is a Muslim who has taken vows of poverty and leads an austere life. Of these there are various orders, some of whom are known from their fantastic practices, such as the dancing, whirling or howling dervishes.

Comprehension

1 What is it about old Istanbul that is so full of melancholy? Why does the writer celebrate this?

2 What reasons does Pamuk give for preferring darkness to the light of day?

3 What makes you aware that Istanbul was once a much grander city than it is now?

4 How is Istanbul's old city slowly disappearing?

Venetians are not at all attuned to the rhythm of
the wheel. That is for other places, places with
motor vehicles. Ours is the rhythm of the
15 Adriatic. The rhythm of the sea. In Venice
the rhythm flows along with the tide,
and the tide changes every six hours.'

Count Marcello inhaled deeply.
'How do you see a bridge?'

20 'Pardon me?' I asked. 'A bridge?'

'Do you see a bridge as an obstacle
– as just another set of steps to
climb to get from one side of the
canal to the other? We Venetians
25 do not see bridges as obstacles. To
us bridges are transitions. We go
over them very slowly. They are
part of the rhythm. They are the
links between two parts of a theatre,
30 like changes in scenery, or like the
progression from Act One of a play to
Act Two. Our role changes as we go over
bridges. We cross from one reality ... to
another reality. From one street ... to another
35 street. From one setting ... to another setting.'

We were approaching a bridge crossing over Rio di
San Luca into Campo Manin.

'A *trompe l'oeil* painting,' Count Marcello went on 'is a
painting that is so lifelike it doesn't look like a painting at
40 all. It looks like real life, but of course it is not. It is reality
once removed. What, then, is a *trompe l'oeil* painting when it
is reflected in a mirror? Reality twice removed?

'Sunlight on a canal is reflected up through a window on to
the ceiling, then from the ceiling on to a vase, and from the
45 vase on to a glass, or a silver bowl. Which is the real
sunlight? Which is the real reflection? What is true? What is
not true? The answer is not so simple, because the truth can

Word origins

Trompe l'oeil in French means 'to
deceive the eye'. The term is
used to describe a painting that
tricks you into thinking the
painted scene is real.

change. I can change. You can change. That is the Venice effect.'

50 We descended from the bridge into Campo Manin. Other than having come from the deep shade of Calle della Mandola into the bright sunlight of the open square, I felt unchanged. My role, whatever it was, remained the same as it had been before the bridge. I did not of course admit this
55 to Count Marcello. But I looked at him to see if he would acknowledge having undergone any change himself.

He breathed deeply as we walked into Campo Manin. Then, with an air of finality, he said, 'Venetians never tell the truth. We mean precisely the opposite of what we say.'

JOHN BERENDT

Comprehension

1 Venice is famous for the masked parties held during *Carnevale*. What does Count Marcello say about the people of Venice that emphasizes how much Venetians love to pretend to be someone else?

2 Where do the Venetians get their special sense of rhythm from, according to Count Marcello?

3 What other functions do the bridges of Venice have (in addition to providing a way to cross the canals), according to Count Marcello?

4 Describe some of the features of Venice that relate to the visual or performing arts.

10 Finding your place

What does it mean to find your own place in the world?

In this unit you will:

Experience
- Koreans in the USA
- Chinese in Australia
- Syrians in the USA
- Croatia and Bosnia
- the United Kingdom
- an orphan train in nineteenth-century USA

Read
- fiction
- poetry
- autobiography
- a historical novel

Create
- a letter to a magazine
- an analogy
- a reflection

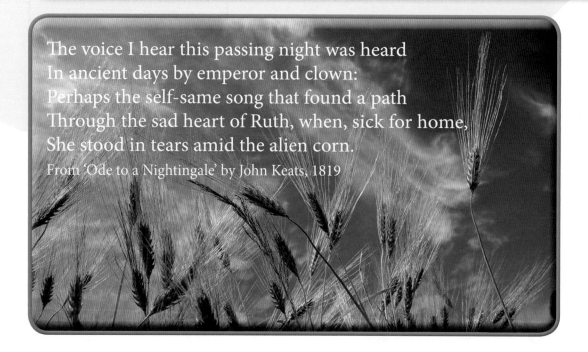

The voice I hear this passing night was heard
In ancient days by emperor and clown:
Perhaps the self-same song that found a path
Through the sad heart of Ruth, when, sick for home,
She stood in tears amid the alien corn.

From 'Ode to a Nightingale' by John Keats, 1819

Finding your way in a changing world is something we all have to deal with at some point in our lives. Growing up is stressful for young people and their families. How much more difficult do you think it is for families who have made their home in another country?

Talking points

1 How do these lines from Keats capture what young people experience when they first come to live in another country?

2 What kinds of pressures does moving country put on families?

Fiction

From *A Step from Heaven* by An Na

Young Ju is a teenager who emigrated from Korea to America with her parents
when she was young. As a child she thought they were on their way to heaven,
but as she grows up the difficulties become more apparent. She finds the
cultural divide between life at home and school increasingly difficult to cope
with. Here, she is trying to persuade her mother to allow her to go to her best
friend's party on the beach.

❧ Becoming too American ❧

It is Amanda's first party. A beach birthday party. I can't go,
Uhmma and Apa do not like it that my best friend is an
American, a girl who might influence me in the wrong
ways. Fast American ways. Supposedly, American girls do
5   not study and they do not think of anyone but themselves.
Uhmma and Apa do not want me to end up like them.

'But Uhmma,' I beg, following her down the hall to the
kitchen. 'It is her birthday.'

'No, Young Ju, you can see her at school and give her your
10 gift then, but you don't need to go to the beach with her.'

'Why?' I ask and slam my body into a chair. 'Why, Uhmma?
What is so wrong with going to the beach?'

'Always "why" with you. Do not let your Apa hear those
kinds of words. Already he has been complaining that you
15 ask too many questions. Young Ju, we will go to the beach
another time,' Uhmma says.

She pulls some scallions out of the refrigerator and rinses
them off in the sink.

'That is not the same,' I cry. 'Amanda needs me at the party. I
20 am her best friend!'

As Uhmma carries the scallions to the cutting board near the
sieve, she gives me a narrow-eyed glance. This is a sore
subject. I change my tactics.

UK	USA
spring onion	scallion

GLOSSARY

Uhmma and *Apa* are the Korean
names for mother and father.

'Yes, I will remember,' Uhmma says.

90 I step out of the car and wave goodbye. Uhmma leans across the passenger seat giving me a finger shake.

'Young Ju, do not forget to give Ah-man-dah the money you borrowed. Be a polite girl and help her parents with the party.'

95 I hold the door, ready to slam it shut.

'Yes, Uhmma,' I say, waving again. 'Bye.'

Uhmma waves back. 'Have a nice time, Young Ju.'

I shut the door and walk away. The station wagon sputters as Uhmma presses on the gas pedal. I know without turning
100 around that there are dark clouds of smoke streaming from the muffler.

AN NA

Comprehension

1 Why is Young Ju's mother so reluctant to accept her daughter's friendship with Amanda?

2 How does Young Ju's father expect her to behave?

3 Which unsuccessful arguments does Young Ju use in her attempts to persuade her mother to allow her to go to the beach party?

4 Explain Young Ju's deception at the end of the text. Why does she lie to her mother?

Writing a letter to a magazine

W Write a letter to the problem page of a magazine. Talk about any difficulties or misunderstandings that might occur in a family relationship. It could be with a parent or a sibling.

- You can use the case studies and the characters from these stories or make up a situation of your own.
- Use the appropriate language to express the different points of view of a parent or a brother or sister. Use emotive and expressive language to explain your frustrations, and how much you want to improve the relationship.

Autobiography

From *Unpolished Gem* by Alice Pung

Alice Pung, the writer of the following text, was born in Melbourne in Australia. Her Chinese-Cambodian parents had made the perilous journey to escape from Cambodia's 'killing fields' when the country was ruled by Pol Pot in the 1970s just before she was born. Alice identifies with both worlds: the world of her family's history and culture, and the Australian world of school and friends into which she was born. Alice feels secure, but life continues to be a struggle for her mother who does not speak English. Her mother's ambition to 'learn the English' came comparatively late in life. Making up for lost time, it becomes an obsession, and Alice tries to help her.

Learning English in Australia

ഔ Learning the English ഔ

The quieter I became at school the louder my mother became at home. She was loud because she could not read or speak the secret talk we knew. She could not read because she had been housebound for two decades. And now, over the dinner
5 table, she would watch as my father and his children littered their language with English terms, until every second word was in the foreign tongue. We hardly noticed the food which she had prepared for us, so engrossed were we in our babble. She sat there staring at us, trying to make sense of these
10 aliens at her table.

'Migrants don't assimilate,' I was told by classmates in politics class. 'They all come here and stick together, and don't bother to learn the language'. But I remembered when my mother bundled all four of us into the car after school.
15 'Agheare,' she told me. 'Look at the map. Find this place for me. Your father gave me the address. I am going to learn the English. I am going to learn it now, no matter what.' We did not even change out of our uniforms, there was no time. My mother decided that if she knew the English, all her problems

Wordpool

housebound (line 4)

to litter (5)

to be engrossed in babble (8)

to assimilate (11)

felt (26)

flannel (27)

incredulously (33)

blazer (50)

discreetly (55)

An Australian possum

20 would be solved, she would be able to do anything in this new country. Most of all, she would be able to enter the world of her children's minds.

We pulled up in front of a community centre and
25 were met by a kind woman with a lilting British accent, hair like a soft grey felt hat on her head, grey flannel scarf and kind grey eyes. She looked like an old wise possum and she invited us all into the centre for coffee before our discussion.
30 My mother's heart melted. We all sat round a table strewn with newspapers and books.

'So it says here that your mother is forty,' said the woman incredulously.

Until then, I didn't even know my mother's age. I asked her,
35 and she nodded.

'Unbelievable! She looks twenty!' I repeated this to my mother. She signed up for the class straightaway.

My mother asked us to speak to her in English. I did so, slowly and carefully. I asked her questions: 'How are you?
40 How was your day?' But because these were questions Chinese children never asked their parents, even if she had enough words to answer me, she would not have known how. 'Stop asking me crazy, pointless questions,' she said, 'and let me learn something useful!'

45 'Alright, Ma. What do you want to learn? What do you want to talk about?'

'You tell me! You're the teacher now!' She looked at me as if I had all the answers and was keeping them from her from some perverse whim, as if I had them hidden in the inside
50 pocket of my blazer.

The migrants in her class were all at different levels, and my mother could not understand the worksheets. She dumped all her notebooks and worksheets on the floor of her room.

GLOSSARY

A **possum** is a marsupial (a mammal which carries its baby in a pouch) which is found in North and Central America, Australia and New Zealand. They are nocturnal animals ('nocturnal' means that they are more active at night).

Agheare is the writer's Chinese name.

Ginseng is a plant the root of which is used in Chinese medicine.

The roots of ginseng

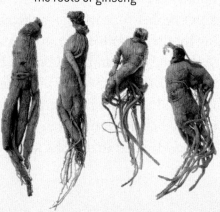

55 'Well, this stuff might be too hard,' I said, discreetly shoving the piles of paper under her bed. 'Why don't you start from the very beginning?' I picked up my five-year-old sister's school reader. 'Pat is ... a ... cat', my mother read. 'He is a black and white cat.' Her fingers, gnarled as just-dug-up

60 ginseng, pointed at each word. She could read the whole book through not once, not twice, but three times. She sighed a big sigh. 'Ah, it's no use. No use! It is all useless, I don't understand a thing.'

'But Ma, you just read the whole book through three times.'

65 'No, I didn't!'

'Yes, you did!'

She turned to the middle pages and pointed. 'I don't know what it says. I just memorised the whole thing when you first read it out to me. Don't teach me any more. Go off and

70 study.'

ALICE PUNG

Comprehension

1 Why did the writer's mother feel that her family had become 'aliens at her table'? (line 10)

2 What does this extract explain about the success and failure of the family's assimilation into Australian society?

3 How would 'learning the English' help the writer's mother?

4 What qualities in the mother's character make it difficult for her to learn English?

Looking closely

1 Explain the feelings of the writer's mother a) at the dinner table (lines 5–10), b) when she was with the community centre teacher (24–37), and c) when the writer tried to teach her. (38–50)

2 What is 'assimilation'? (line 11) How does this extract contradict the point made about migrants refusing to assimilate?

3 Why are the questions the writer asks her mother inappropriate? (lines 39–44)

4 What is a 'perverse whim'? (line 49) How does it help to explain the confused relationship between mother and daughter?

5 Explain the following two similes: a) 'like an old wise possum' (line 28) and b) 'gnarled as just-dug-up ginseng'. (lines 59–60)

Talking points

1 What kind of problems are the families in *Learning the English* and *Becoming too American* experiencing?

2 What do you think the family members could do to improve the situations in the two texts?

3 What special difficulties do the children of migrants face in their teenage years? What divided loyalties do they experience?

Poem

The writer of the following poem describes the experience of her family, who left Damascus in Syria for a life in Utah in the Midwest of America.

ೞ The Roc ೞ

Here's my mom and dad leaving
    all familiar signposts: Damascus, the streets they knew,
    measurement of time in mosque sounds,
    the regular scrape of heavy wooden shutters,
5   the daily boiling and cooling of fresh milk.
    Anyone back home who had no phone fell off
    the disc of their new world: tomato-cart man,
    schoolchildren in skittish flocks. Crazy Fat' ma
    the Goatwoman, all the newly married cousins,
10 the porter at the door they left behind.

Here they are crossing the world,
hoisting up all they know like a sail,
landing in Utah. The time is March 15, 1971.

They know nothing about America:
15   how to grocery shop,
    how to open a bank account,
    how the milk comes, thin glass bottles
    on tin chinking them awake,
what 'you bet' or 'sure thing' meant
20   in real spoken English, outside
    the London-grammar books so creased,
    so carefully underlined. It was,
    my mother said, as if a monstrous bird
had seized them up and dropped
25   them in a fantastic terrain.

    Here's my mother studying
    the instructions on the coin-
    box of a laundry machine,
    enrolling us in kindergarten,
30 tape-recording her college lectures so
    that she could play, replay, decode
    the stream of alien phonemes into words.

GLOSSARY

The **Roc** (also known as the **Rukh**) is the bird of Arabian mythology. Marco Polo described rocs living in Madagascar, and Sinbad the Sailor in *The Arabian Nights* described seeing one which 'blotted out the sun' on his second voyage after he had found the 'great white dome' of a gigantic egg. The roc was said to feed its young on elephants.

A **phoneme** is a linguistic term for a unit of sound that cannot be broken down further.

Wordpool

disc (line 7)

skittish (8)

terrain (25)

to decode (31)

phoneme (32)

to stake (36)

subsidize (44)

vertigo (55)

transmission (59)

epic (62)

to pulsate (62)

talon (66)

That's her refolding foil, stretching the little
       budget over the month, making the
35   ten-cent toys our treasures of Sinbad.

       Here's my father staking
       his life's savings on one semester.
He works hard and at the end of the term,
       on the day before the last dollar
40   of the life savings is gone,
       he walks into the Chair's office
       and the Chair gives him a job teaching.
Other friendly natives explain
       subsidized student housing,
45   coupons, and the good places to find
       bargain basement merchandise.

       The pilgrims were so happy
at being shown how to survive here
       after the first long winter,
50   they had a feast. That's mom,
       laughing at the strange loaf of bread.
       There's dad holding up the new world coffee
in its funny striped boxes. That's us,
       small, weightless, wobbly
55   with the vertigo of the newly landed
       voyager.

       Here they are, mom and dad,
       telephoning back home, where the folks
       gather around the transmission
60   as if it was from the moon.
       The phone call to Syria was
       for epic events only. The line pulsates
as if with the beating of enormous wings.
They shout and shout into the receiver
65   as if the other end were ages
       and ages away. Spiny talon
       digs into rock.

Mohja Kahf

The Roc, which fed its young on elephants

UK   USA

There are a number of different words for mother and father in English. In the United States you might call your parents 'mom and dad', but in the UK or Australia it would be more likely to be 'mum and dad'.

In the US, dates are written in this order:
March 15, 1971 or 03/15/71.

In the UK, this date would be written as:
15 March 1971 or 15/03/71.

175

When do new places present a particular challenge?

Many people don't like change, and like to stay in the same place all their lives. This might seem dull or unadventurous. But for some people that is all the stimulation they need. Moving away from what is safe and familiar can be a wrenching experience.

Fiction

From *The Curious Incident of the Dog in the Night-time* by Mark Haddon

This excerpt from a novel by Mark Haddon describes the world from the point of view of Christopher John Francis Boone, a 15-year-old boy with autism living in Swindon, Wiltshire, in England. He is very logically-minded and good at mathematics, but he has problems relating to people and dealing with new situations. Siobhan is Christopher's teacher and his friend. He reflects on conversations they have had as a way to help him work things out, and better adapt to the world he lives in. She encourages him to write things down.

❧ Standing in a Field ❧

I see everything. That is why I don't like new places. If I am in a place I know like home, or school, or the bus, or the shop, or the street, I have seen almost everything in it beforehand and all I have to do is to look at the things that
5 have changed or moved. For example, one week, the **Shakespeare's Globe** poster had fallen down in the classroom at school and you could tell because it had been put back slightly to the right and there were three little circles of Blu-Tack stain on the wall down the left-hand side of the
10 poster. And the next day someone had graffitied **CROW APTOK** to lamppost 437 in our street which is the one outside number 35.

But most people are lazy. They never look properly. They do what is called *glancing* which is the same word for bumping
15 off something and carrying on in almost the same direction, e.g. when a snooker ball glances off another snooker ball. And the information in their head is really simple. For example, if they are in the countryside, it might be:

I am standing in a field that is full of grass.

Wordpool

to graffiti (line 10)

cooker (29)

scenic (36)

clarification (72)

processor (91)

computer program (102)

capacity (107)

GLOSSARY

A person with an **autistic spectrum disorder** often has difficulty communicating and socially interacting with other people, and enjoys repetitive activities. People with autism often focus on developing very specific interests and expertise in a technical field of knowledge.

Snooker is a game, played with balls on a billiard table.

An **economist** works in the field of economics, a branch of knowledge concerned with managing finance, production and the consumption of goods.

A **logician** works in the branch of philosophy that deals with the principles of logical thought and scientific method.

20 There are some cows in the fields.
It is sunny with a few clouds.
There are some flowers in the grass.
There is a village in the distance.
There is a fence at the edge of the field and it has
25 a gate in.

And then they would stop noticing anything
because they would be thinking something else
like, 'Oh, it is very beautiful here,' or, 'I'm
worried that I might have left the gas cooker
30 on,' or, 'I wonder if Julie has given birth yet.'

But if I am standing in a field in the countryside
I notice everything. For example, I remember
standing in a field on Thursday 15th June 1994
because Father and Mother and I were driving to Dover to
35 get a ferry to France and we did what Father called *Taking
the scenic route* which means going by little roads and
stopping for lunch in a pub garden, and I went into a field
with cows in, looked at the field and I noticed these things.

There are 19 cows in the field, 15 of which are black and
40 white and 4 of which are brown and white.

There is a village in the distance which has 31 visible houses
and a church with a square tower and not a spire.

There are ridges in the field which means that in medieval
times it was what is called a *ridge and furrow* field and
45 people who lived in the village would have a ridge each to do
farming on.

There is an old plastic bag from Asda in the hedge, and a
squashed Coca-cola can with a snail on it, and a long piece
of orange string.

50 The north-east corner of the field is highest and the south-
west corner is lowest (I had a compass because we were
going on holiday and I wanted to know where Swindon was
when we were in France) and the field is folded downwards
slightly along the line between these two corners so that the

55   north-west and south-east corners are slightly lower than they would be if the field was a flat inclined plane.

I can see three different types of grass and two colours of flowers in the grass.

The cows are mostly facing uphill. And there were 31 more
60   things in this list of things I noticed but Siobhan said I didn't need to write them all down. And it means that it is very tiring if I am in a new place because I see all these things, and if someone asked me afterwards what the cows looked like, I could ask which one, and I could do a drawing of them at
65   home and say that a particular cow had patterns on it like this (draws a picture of a cow).

And I realise that I told a lie in **Chapter 13** because I said, 'I cannot tell jokes', because I do know three jokes that I can tell and I understand and one of them is about a cow, and
70   Siobhan said I didn't have to go back and change what I wrote in **Chapter 14** because it doesn't matter because it is not a lie, just a clarification.

And this is the joke. There are three men on a train. One of them is an economist and one of them is a logician and one
75   of them is a mathematician. And they have just crossed the border into Scotland (I don't know why they are going to Scotland) and they see a brown cow standing in a field from the window of the train (and the cow is standing parallel to the train).

80   And the economist says, 'Look, the cows in Scotland are brown.'

And the logician says, 'No. There are cows in Scotland of which one, at least, is brown.'

And the mathematician says, 'No. There is at least one cow
85   in Scotland of which one side appears to be brown.'

And it is funny because economists are not real scientists, and because logicians think more clearly, but mathematicians are best.

Looking closely

1   Why does Christopher find new places stressful? (paragraph 1)

2   What kinds of things does Christopher focus on, when he records what he sees? List the details of what he sees in the cow field. (lines 39–56)

3   What is 'a clarification'? (line 72) How is it different from a lie or a falsehood?

4   What does Christopher compare his mind to when he gets overloaded with too much information?

5   What makes Christopher impatient with other people who do not share his way of looking at the world? What does he think of them?

Journal

Do you ever get annoyed with people who don't see things the way you do? Write about a funny situation you have experienced.

90 And when I am in a new place, because I see everything, it is like when a computer is doing too many things at the same time and the central processor unit is blocked up and there isn't any space left to think about other things. And when I am in a new place and there are lots of people there it is even harder because people are not like cows and flowers and

95 grass and they can talk to you and do things that you don't expect, so you have to notice everything that is in the place, and also you have to notice things that might happen as well. And sometimes, when I am in a new place and there are lots of people there it is like a computer crashing and I have to

100 close my eyes and put my hands over my ears and groan, which is like pressing CTRL + ALT + DEL and shutting down programs and turning the computer off and rebooting so that I can remember what I am doing and where I am meant to be going.

105 And that is why I am good at chess and maths and logic, because most people are almost blind and they don't see most things and there is lots of spare capacity in their heads that's filled with things which aren't connected and are silly, like, 'I'm worried that I might have left the gas cooker on.'

Mark Haddon

Comprehension

1 Why does Christopher focus so much on the detail? Why is he distrustful of conventional ideas of beauty in the landscape?

2 What does the joke reveal about Christopher?

3 How else do we know that Christopher loves mathematics?

4 What does Christopher mean, when he calls most people 'blind'? What is Christopher blind to?

5 Why do you think Christopher may appear to other people to be unsympathetic? Why does he have difficulty relating to other people?

Toolkit

Use of i.e. and e.g.

These contractions are often used in technical descriptions such as you might find in 'Standing in a Field':

• i.e. comes from the Latin *id est* and stands for 'that is'. It is used in place of 'in other words'.

• e.g. comes from the Latin *exempli gratia* which means 'for the sake of an example'.

Write two sentences using i.e. and two using e.g. **W**

Extension read

From *Rodzina* by Karen Cushman

This extract from the novel *Rodzina* is set in the nineteenth century. It is about a group of orphaned children who travel on an orphan train to the Midwest of the United States of America in order to find a placement there. Although fictional, it is based on the real experience of children who were 'placed out' by the many charitable agencies operating in the nineteenth century to find homes for orphans. The narrator is a 12-year-old Polish orphan called Rodzina who, while struggling with her own doubts and fears, puts on a brave face for the younger children.

After travelling from Chicago, through Illinois, Iowa, Nebraska and now Wyoming, the party of children is dwindling and the anxiety of those children still unplaced is growing. They are now heading for Cheyenne, where a poster like this one has been sent in advance:

Wordpool

dipper (4)

dreary (6)

to reckon (14)

stubbly (18)

prairie (19)

a jeweled sceptre (89)

WANTED
HOMES FOR CHILDREN

A COMPANY OF TWENTY-TWO HOMELESS CHILDREN OF VARIOUS AGES AND SEXES, HAVING BEEN

THROWN FRIENDLESS ON THE WORLD, WILL BE AT THE CHEYENNE SCHOOLHOUSE ON APRIL 2, 1881, FOR THE PURPOSE OF FINDING THEM NEW HOMES.

PERSONS TAKING THESE CHILDREN MUST BE APPROVED BY THE AGENTS WHO ARE ACCOMPANYING THEM AND MUST PROMISE KIND TREATMENT, GOOD MORAL TRAINING, DECENT CLOTHES, AND A FAIR COMMON SCHOOL EDUCATION.

AN ADDRESS WILL BE MADE BY THE PLACING-OUT AGENT,

LEONARD R. SZPROT.

PIE AND COFFEE
WILL BE SERVED

∽ Cheyenne ∾

Next morning I bumped into Mickey Dooley at the water bucket. 'Know what kind of fish live in a water bucket?' He asked, his eyes as usual looking here and there at the same time. He didn't wait for an answer but waved the dipper at
5 me and said, 'Wet fish. Get it? Wet fish.'

I wanted to keep on thinking my dreary thoughts and not be interrupted with fish jokes. 'Why do you keep joking about nothing all the time?' I asked him. 'We're coming up to Cheyenne, where we'll be sold like chicken feed to farmers.
10 Aren't you worried?'

'Water you mean?' he asked.

'Why—' I began, and then stopped my questions. His left eye had managed to quit its wandering and look right at me. I could see sadness there. Why, I reckoned he was just as
15 worried as I was. He just couldn't say so. I figured the least I could do was pretend right along him. 'Wet fish! You sure are one funny fellow, Mickey Dooley, wet fish.'

Back at my seat I watched out the window. The flat, stubbly prairie looked like Papa's face when he needed a shave. Here
20 and there were herds of animals Chester thought were antelope. Or moose. Or elk. Sure weren't buffalo, he said.

Nellie came and leaned against my legs. 'I don't want to go west,' she said. 'Spud said the west is full of murderers and guns and wildfires. I'm plumb scared of the west.'

25 'No. He's wrong. West is a good place to go,' I told her. I lifted her up and settled her between Lacey and me. 'My mama used to tell me a story about the west, when we first came from Poland, heading west to a whole new country. Seems there was a—'

30 'Once upon a time,' said Nellie, nose dripping on my sleeve. 'That's how stories start.'

'Okay, then. Once upon a time in a town far away in Poland lived a tailor named Matuschanski. He was a very tall man

UK	USA
pavement	sidewalk
jewelled	jeweled
traveller	traveler

(In US spelling, the second 'l' is only used when there is a stress on the last syllable.)

Children in a city street, photographed in 1890

Two young farm boys, photographed in 1890

185

with a very long nose and a very long beard. And he was so
thin, he could pass through the eye of his own needle, so thin
he fell through the cracks in the sidewalk, so thin he could
eat only noodles, one at a time. But he was a kind man and a
very good tailor.'

Lacey snuggled closer to Nellie so that she could listen, until
all three of us were pressed right up against the window.

I went on. 'One day a gypsy passing through town cut her
foot on a stone. She came to see the tailor, who darned it so
neatly there was no scar. As payment, she read his fortune in
his palm: "If you leave this town on a Sunday," she said,
"and walk always westward, you will reach a place where
you will be a king."

Chester and Mickey Dooley came and sat on the floor by my
feet. "Well," said the tailor, "I will never know whether or
not she was right unless I go." And so Pan Matuschanski
packed up a bundle with a needle, a thousand miles of
thread, and a pair of scissors.'

'A thousand miles of thread?' asked Chester. 'Im-possible.'

'Possible in this story. Just listen. All the tailor knew of west
is that it was where the sun set, and so he walked that way.
After seven days he reached the kingdom of Splatt.'

'Now Splatt had troubles. The King had died, and it was
raining. It was pouring. Everywhere else it was sunny, but
over Splatt it was raining and had been ever since the king
died.

'The townspeople moaned, "Oh, who will stop the rain? It
comes in our windows and chimneys, floods our roads,
washes away our flowers, drowns our fish."'

'Drowned fish!' Spud and Joe, who had joined the bunch at
my feet, laughed so hard at that they fell over in a heap,
kicking and punching each other. Sammy jumped up and
separated the two, made Joe sit down next to him, and
motioned for me to go on. I never before saw Sammy stop
anyone from fighting. A small miracle.

'The princess of Splatt said, "I promise my hand in marriage
70   to the person who can stop the rain."'

'The tailor liked the idea of marrying a princess and
becoming king. He thought and thought. Hmm. "I know!"
he shouted finally. "Your king was so great and mighty that
when he died and went to Heaven, he made a great and
75   mighty hole in the sky. It will rain forever unless that hole is
sewn up."'

'Never happen,' said Spud.

'Happened here,' I said. 'So Pan Matuschanski had the
townspeople take all the ladders in the town, tie them
80   together, and lean them against the sky. Then he took his
needle and his thousand miles of thread and climbed up and
up and up. When he got to the sky, sure enough, there was a
huge hole in it. He went to work and sewed and sewed. Two
days later, fingers stiff and back sore, he climbed down the
85   ladder.

'The sun was shining in Splatt. "Long live the king," said the
mayor, handing him a golden crown while the townsfolk all
cheered.

"And," said the princess, handing him a jeweled sceptre,
90   "long live my husband." And he did.'

When I finished, Nellie was asleep against my shoulder.
Lacey was sleeping too. And Mickey Dooley, Spud, Chester,
and Joe. 'May we all be kings in the west,' I said with a great
sigh, as I leaned back in my seat. 'Or at least safe and happy.'
95   And I slept too.

KAREN CUSHMAN

Comprehension

1 What does the conversation at the water bucket reveal about Rodzina and Mickey Dooley?

2 Why do you think Rodzina and the other orphans are reluctant to travel out west for a placement with a family?

3 Why does Rodzina put her negative feelings aside when she talks to the other children?

3 Why do you think she tells them the story about the tailor Matuschanski?

Rodzina and the other orphans travelled in a train like this one across the Midwest of America

Acknowledgments

The author and publisher are grateful for permission to reprint the following copyright material:

Ethan Aames: extract from interview with Georgie Henley and James McAvoy as posted on CineCon site 12 August 2005, www.cinecon.com, reprinted by permission of Cinema Confidential.

Richard Adams: extract from Watership Down (Puffin, 2007), reprinted by permission of David Higham Associates.

Aravind Adiga: extract from The White Tiger (Atlantic Books, 2008), reprinted by permission of the publishers.

Allan Ahlberg: 'Billy McBone' from Heard It in the Playground (Viking, 1989), copyright © Allan Ahlberg 1989, reprinted by permission of Penguin Books Ltd.

Sherman Alexie: extract from The Absolutely True Diary of a Part-Time Indian (Andersen Press, 2008), copyright © Sherman Alexie 2007, reprinted by permission of the publishers, Little Brown and Company, The Hachette Book Group and The Random House Group Ltd.

Isaac Asimov: extract from 'Reason' in I, Robot (HarperCollins, 1993) first published 1950, reprinted by permission of Random House Inc.

Leo Benedictus: extracts from profile 'Sky High: The Air Traffic Controller', The Guardian 18.10.2008, reprinted by permission of Guardian News and Media.

Alan Bennett: extracts from Act 1 of The History Boys (Faber, 2004), reprinted by permission of Faber and Faber Ltd.

John Berendt: opening extract from The City of Falling Angels (Hodder & Stoughton, 2005), reprinted by permission of the publishers.

James Berry: 'Old Slave Villages' from Windrush Songs (Bloodaxe, 2007), reprinted by permission of Bloodaxe Books.

E R Braithwaite: extract from To Sir with Love (Vintage, 2005), reprinted by permission of David Higham Associates Ltd.

Anthony Bourdain: extract from Kitchen Confidential (Bloomsbury, 2000), reprinted by permission of Bloomsbury USA.

Karen Cushman: extract from Rodzina (Clarion Books, 2003), copyright © Karen Cushman 2003reprinted by permission of Curtis Brown Ltd and Clarion Books, an imprint of Houghton Mifflin Harcourt Publishing Company. All Rights Reserved.

Leon Garfield: extract from Smith (Constable, 1967), reprinted by permission of Johnson & Alcock on behalf of the Estate of Leon Garfield.

Graphic Maps: population statistic tables from www.worldatlas.com, reprinted by permission of Graphic Maps.

Mark Haddon: extract from The Curious Incident of the Dog in the Nighttime (David Fickling Books, 2003), reprinted by permission of The Random House Group Ltd and Aitken Alexander Associates.

Gaye Hiçyilmaz: extract from Against the Storm (Faber, 1998), reprinted by permission of Faber and Faber Ltd.

Khaled Hosseini: extract from The Kite Runner (Bloomsbury, 2003), reprinted by permission of the publishers, Bloomsbury Publishing plc and Penguin Group USA.

Langston Hughes: 'I Too Sing America' from The Collected Poems of Langston Hughes edited by Arnold Rampersad (Alfred Knopf, 2007), reprinted by permission of David Higham Associates Ltd and Alfred A Knopf, a division of Random House Inc.

Holbrook Jackson: 'Town', first published in 1913, from Occasions: A Volume of Essays upon Divers Subjects (Grant Richards Ltd, 1922), reprinted by permission of The Society of Authors as the Literary Representative of the Estate of Holbrook Jackson.

Elizabeth Jennings: 'Friends' from New Collected Poems edited by Michael Schmidt (Carcanet, 2002), reprinted by permission of David Higham Associates Ltd.

Brian Jones: 'About Friends' from Spitfire on the Northern Line (Chatto & Windus, 1975), reprinted by permission of The Random House Group Ltd

Mohja Kahf: 'The Roc' from The Poetry of Arab Women: A Contemporary Anthology edited by Nathalie Handal (Interlink Books, 2001), reprinted by permission of the publishers.

Martin Luther King Jr: extracts from 'I have a Dream..', copyright © 1963 Martin Luther King Jr, copyright renewed 1991 by Coretta Scott King, reprinted by arrangement with the heirs of the Estate of Martin Luther King Jr, c/o Writers House as agent for the Proprietor, New York, NY.

C S Lewis: extract from The Lion, The Witch and the Wardrobe (HarperCollins Childrens' Books, 2007), copyright © C S Lewis Pte Ltd 1950, reprinted by permission of The CS Lewis Company.

Patricia McCormick: extract from 'If only Papa hadn't Danced' from Free? Stories Celebrating Human Rights (Walker Books for Amnesty International, 2009), reprinted by permission of Amnesty International.

Nelson Mandela: extract from A Long Walk to Freedom (Little, Brown, 1994), copyright © Nelson Rolihlahla Mandela 1994, reprinted by permission of the publishers, Little, Brown Book Group.

Vesna Maric: extract from Bluebird: A Memoir (Granta, 2009), reprinted by permission of the publishers, Granta Books and Soft Skull Press.

Adrian Mitchell: 'Secret Country' from Love Songs of World War Three (Allison & Busby, 1989), reprinted by permission of United Agents on behalf of the author's Estate.

An Na: extract from A Step from Heaven (Allen & Unwin, 2002), reprinted by permission of HarperCollins Publishers.

Lee Ann Obringer and Jonathan Strickland: extract from 'How Asimo works', from www.science.howstuffworks.com/ reprinted by permission of How Stuff Works.

George Orwell: extract from Down and Out in Paris and London (first published 1933), copyright © George Orwell 1933, renewed 1961 by Sonia Pitt-Rivers, reprinted by permission of A M Heath & Co Ltd on behalf of Bill Hamilton as the Literary Executor of the Estate of the late Sonia Brownell Orwell and Secker & Warburg Ltd, and of Houghton Mifflin Harcourt Publishing Company.

Orhan Pamuk: extract from Istanbul: Memories of a City translated by Maureen Freely (Faber, 2005), reprinted by permission of Faber and Faber Ltd.

Doris Pilkington: extract from Rabbit-Proof Fence (University of Queensland Press, 1996), copyright © Doris Pilkington-Nugi Garimara 1996, reproduced by permission of the publishers, Miramax Books c/o Hyperion. All rights reserved.

Alice Pung: extract from Unpolished Gem (Portobello, 2008), copyright © Alice Pung 2008, reprinted by permission of Portobello Books, Black Inc. Australia and Penguin Group USA.

Kocho Racin: 'Tobacco Pickers' translated by Broz Koneski from The Song Atlas: A Book of World Poetry edited by John Gallas (Carcanet, 2002), reprinted by permission of the publisher.

Taufiq Ralat: lines from 'Arrival of the Monsoon' from A Dragonfly in the Sun edited by Muneeza Shamsie (OUP Pakistan, 1998), reprinted by permission of Oxford University Press Pakistan.

Antoine de St Exupery: extract from Southern Mail translated by Curtis Cate (Penguin, 2000), reprinted by permission of The Random House Group Ltd

Carl Sandburg: 'Fog' from The Complete Poems of Carl Sandburg (Houghton Mifflin, 2003), reprinted by permission of Houghton Mifflin Harcourt Publishing Company.

Alexander Solzhenitsyn: One Day in the Life of Ivan Denisovich Shukhov translated by Ralph Parker (Penguin Classics, 2000), reprinted by permission of Penguin Books Ltd.

Marin Sorescu: 'Playing Icarus' from The Biggest Egg in the World (Bloodaxe, 1987), reprinted by permission of Bloodaxe Books.

Louisa Waugh: extract from 'Letters from Tsengal', Mongolia 1998 in Letters frm the Edge: 12 Women of the World Write Home edited by Chris Brazier (New Internationalist, 2008), reprinted by permission of the publishers.

Damon Weaver: interview with President Barack Obama on election night from abcnews.go.com/GMA/ reprinted by permission of ABC News.

H G Wells: extract from The Time Machine (Penguin, 2007), reprinted by permission of A P Watt Ltd on behalf of the Literary Executors of the Estate of H G Wells.

William Carlos Williams: 'Landscape with the Fall of Icarus' from The Collected Poems: Volume II, 1939-1962 (Carcanet, 2000), copyright © William Carlos Williams 1962, reprinted by permission of the publishers, New Directions Publishing Corp. and Carcanet Press Ltd.

Although we have made every effort to trace and contact all copyright holders before publication this has not been possible in all cases. If notified, the publisher will rectify any errors or omissions at the earliest opportunity.

Linda Sue Park: extract from A Single Shard (OUP, 2001), copyright © Linda Sue Park 2001, reprinted by permission of Oxford University Press.

Bill Paterson, extract from Tales from the Back Green (Hodder & Stoughton, 2008), copyright © Bill Paterson 2008, reprinted by permission of the publishers and David Godwin Associates Ltd

Suzanne Fisher Staples, adapted extract from Daughter of the Wind (Walker Books, 2002), text copyright © Suzanne Fisher Staples 1989, reprinted by permission of the publishers, Walker Books Ltd, London SE11 5HJ and Random House, Inc.

Ingalls Wilder: extract from Little House on the Prairie (Egmont, 2000), copyright Laura Ingalls Wilder 1953, © renewed 1963 by Roger L MacBride, reprinted by permission of the publishers.

The Publisher would like to thank the following for permission to reproduce photographs:

Front cover photo Digital Vision/Alamy; p6a James Thew/Shutterstock; p6b JoLin/Shutterstock; p6c Fedor A. Sidorov/Shutterstock; p8 Tracy Whiteside/Shutterstock; p9a North Wind Picture Archives/Alamy; p9b BORTEL Pavel/Shutterstock; p10 ArchMan/Shutterstock; p11 Kuttig - People/Alamy; p12a Ali Ender Birer/Shutterstock; p12b OUP Captureweb; p12c ZQFotography/Shutterstock; p12d Phase4Photography/Shutterstock; p13a Condor36/Shutterstock; p13b Vladimir V. Georgievskiy/Shutterstock; p15 Steve Skjold/Alamy; p17 WALT DISNEY PICTURES/BRAY,PHI; p21 Merrilld/Dreamstime; p22 Redshift Photography/Alamy; p23 Eadam/Dreamstime; p24 WALT DISNEY PICTURES/VINET,PI; p28a traff/Shutterstock; p28b Viacheslav Gorelik/Shutterstock; p29a Tiero/Dreamstime; p29b: ClassicStock/Alamy; p29c Keith Dannemiller/Alamy; p29d Ton Koene/Alamy; p29e Blend Image/OUP; p30 Splashuk/splashnews.com; p31 Press Association Images; p33 Matthew Jacques/Shutterstock; p35 JJ pixs/Shutterstock; p36a Podfoto/Shutterstock; p36b Darryl Sleath/Shutterstock; p36c Douglas Freer/Shutterstock; p37a andras_csontos/Shutterstock; p37b Lebrecht Music and Arts Photo Library/Alamy; p38 Lebrecht Music and Arts Photo Library/Alamy; p39 Serg64/Shutterstock; p40 Peter Johnson/Corbis; p42 AFP/Getty images; p43 Getty Images; p44 COLUMBIA PICTURES/Album/AKG; p48a Vibrant Image Studio/Shutterstock; p48b Alex Staroseltsev/Shutterstock; p49 Caricature of Jules Verne (1828-1905) from 'Men of Today', c. 1880 (colour litho), Gill, Andre (1840-85)/Collection Kharbine-Tapabor, Paris, France/The Bridgeman Art Library; p50a akg-images/Erich Lessing; p50b akg-images/Erich Lessing; p53 Pictorial Press Ltd/Alamy; p54a B. G. Smith/Shutterstock; p54b 2009fotofriends/Shutterstock; p55 akva/Shutterstock; p56a The Mountains of Mystery, from 'Incredible Journeys',1975(gouache on paper), English School, (20th century)/Private Collection/Look and Learn/The Bridgeman Art Library; p56b INTERFOTO/Alamy; p56c Bibliothèque nationale de France; p57a Thomas Cook Archive/Illustrated London News Ltd/Mary Evans; p57b Thomas Cook Archive/Illustrated London News Ltd/Mary Evans p58c Miramax/Everett/Rex Features; p59a Kgrahamjourneys/Dreamstime; p61a Alan Robert Jupp/Shutterstock; p61b Bigstock; p62 Clearviewstock/Shutterstock; p64a Dave Sonnier/Shutterstock; p64b Yan Zommer/Shutterstock; p64c wona Grodzka/Shutterstock; p65a 'The Wealth of England: the Bessemer Process of Making Steel', 1895 (oil on canvas), Titcomb, William Holt Yates (1858-1930)/ Kelham Island Industrial Museum, Sheffield, UK/The Bridgeman Art Library; p65b Photodisc/OUP; p66 Picture Contact/Alamy; p69a Vario images GmbH & Co.KG/ Alamy; p69b Roger Bamber/Alamy; p71 Tom Arne Hanslien/Alamy; p72 Mary Evans Picture Library/Alamy; p74 Edwin Remsberg/Alamy; p75 Mary Evans Picture Library/Alamy; p77 akg-images; p78a Hernan H. Hernandez A./Shutterstock; p78b Faberfoto/Shutterstock; p79 Bigstock; p81 Hansjoerg Richter/IStockphoto; p82 Adrian Arbib/Alamy; p84 RIA Novosti/Alamy; p87 akg-images/RIA Novosti; p88 IML Image Group Ltd/Alamy; p89 Mary Evans Picture Library/CHRISTINE HINZE; p90 Mrs. Francis E. W. Harper (engraving), American School, (19th century)/Newberry Library, Chicago, Illinois, USA/The Bridgeman Art Library; p95 OUP Captureweb; p96 Robwatership/Alamy; p97 Rebecca Anne/Shutterstock; p98a Mushakesa/shutterstock; p98b Tischenko Irina/Shutterstock; p99a Vlad-Koarov/Etoon.com; p99b Chudo-yudo/Shutterstock; p100 AFP/Getty Images; p101 Pictorial Press Ltd/Alamy; p102 Reynold Brown; p103 photoBeard/Shutterstock; p104 Spectral-Design/Shutterstock; p106a PETER MENZEL/SCIENCE PHOTO LIBRARY; p106b akg-images/PictureContact; p107 akg-images/PictureContact; p109 20TH CENTURY FOX/GERLITZ, AVA; p111 Krol/Shutterstock; p112 serjoe/Shutterstock; p116a Taily/Shutterstock; p116b St. Nick/Shutterstock; p117 Alan Merrigan/Shutterstock; p118a Marek R. Swadzba/Shutterstock; p118b INTERFOTO/Alamy; p119 Netfalls/Shutterstock; p120 Landscape with the Fall of Icarus, c.1555 (oil on canvas), Bruegel, Pieter the Elder (c.1525-69)/Musees Royaux des Beaux-Arts de Belgique, Brussels, Belgium/Giraudon/The Bridgeman Art Library; p122a public domain; p122b public domain; p122c public domain; p121 Andrew Fox/Alamy; p123a Juniors Bildarchiv/Alamy; p123b Daniel Hebert/Shutterstock; p124a Illustrated London News Ltd/Mary Evans; p124b Pictorial Press Ltd/Alamy; p125 Kolosigor/Shutterstock; p126 Underwood & Underwood/Corbis; p127 Reuters/Suhaib Salem; p129a Reuters/Suhaib Salem; p129b MOHAMMED SABER/epa/Corbis; p130a Kushch Dmitry/ Shutterstock; p130b Andrew Chin/Shutterstock; p131a DAN PELED/epa/Corbis; p131b Cocohibb/Dreamstime; p131c Frances A Miller/Shutterstock; p132 INTERFOTO/Alamy; p138 Chantal de bruijne/Shutterstock; p140 Bigstock; p141 Photodisc/OUP; p142a Paul Fleet/Alamy Image; p142b Peter Arnold, Inc./Alamy; p142c MalDix/Shutterstock; p143 Daniel Wiedemann/Shutterstock; p144 Lenalir/Dreamstime; p147 Sonifo/Dreamstime; p148a upthebanner/Shutterstock; p148b javarman/Shutterstock; p149 Florence from Bellosguardo, Brett, John (1831-1902)/Private Collection/The Fine Art Society, London, UK/The Bridgeman Art Library; p150a Marco Rullkoetter/Shutterstock; p150b Ken Welsh/Alamy; p150c Oksana.perkins/Shutterstock; p150d MaxFX/Shutterstock; p150e /Ffooter/Shutterstock; p150f Vinicious Tupinamba/Shutterstock; p150g Sunxuejun/Shutterstock; p150h Steba/Shutterstock; p150i Photodisc/OUP; p151 Adisa/Shutterstock; p152 Mary Evans Picture Library; p155a Garwood & Voigt Antique Maps; p155b Mary Evans Picture Library; p156 Street Scene in Paris,1926 (board), Wood, Christopher(1901-30)/Southampton City Art Gallery, Hampshire, UK/The Bridgeman Art Library; p158 David R. Frazier Photolibrary,Inc./Alamy; p160a akg-images/Suzanne Held; p160b National Geographic/Getty Images; p162a Photos 12/Alamy; p162b Pictorial Press Ltd/Alamy; p163 View of the Grand Canal from the South, the Palazzo Foscari to the right and the Rialto Bridge beyond, Canaletto, Antonio (1697-1768) (after)/Private Collection/Bonhams, London, UK/The Bridgeman Art Library; p164 Kreos/Dreamstime; p165 Raphotography/Dreamstime; p166a Matamu/Shutterstock; p166b Pakhnyuschcha/Shutterstock; p167 Yuri Arcurs/Dreamstime; p171 Howard Davies/Corbis; p172a Dejan Novkovski/Shutterstock; p172b Elena Ray/Shutterstock; p175 The Mighty Roc, Escott, Dan (1928-87)/Private Collection/Look and Learn/The Bridgeman Art Library; p177 LianeM/Shutterstock; p179 Coming Home (oil on board), Hayward, Sara (Contemporary Artist)/Private Collection/The Bridgeman Art Library; p181 Elena Elisseeva/Shutterstock; p183 Yarex/Dreamstime; p184 Javarman/Shutterstock; p185a Roger Voillet/Getty Images; p185b Time & Life Pictures/Getty Images; p187 The Protected Art Archive/Alamy.

The author and publisher are grateful for permission to reprint the following copyright material:

Although we have made every effort to trace and contact all copyright holders before publication this has not been possible in all cases. If notified, the publisher will rectify any errors or omissions at the earliest opportunity.